The Voice in My He

The Voice in My Head
is Perfect

Motor Neurone Disease and Me

Lindy Jones

Ashgrove Publishing
London

I would like to dedicate this book to:

*Gareth, Robbie, Owen, Viv, Karey, Dad, and Scrappy,
whose fishy breath, wagging tail and warm tongue
has kept me going during the past three years.*

*Also, to the wonderful Palliative Care Team at the North
London Hospice and all the friends and ex-students
who continue to visit, text, and e-mail.*

*And to Keith, of course, whose faith in my writing
made this book possible.*

Lindy Jones, November 2013
www.lindyjones.co.uk

Contents

•

1.	Emily Brontë and a Walk in the Woods	7
2.	Appointments with Doctor Death	13
3.	Inside the Blair Witch's Cottage	23
4.	The Last Bite is the Deepest	29
5.	Therapy	37
6.	Trees, Leaves, and Peanut Butter Sandwiches	45
7.	Pollyanna has left the Building	51
8.	The PEG Lady	61
9.	Dear Body	67
10.	Medical Procedures	69
11.	The Patient	75
12.	The Dying Line	85
13.	Just My Imagination	89
14.	Keeping it in the Family	93
15.	Grandma	101
16.	A Guided Tour of My Childhood Home	107
17.	Every Breath I Take	119
18.	The Making of a Teacher	125
19.	The Ride of My Life	133
20.	I Will Survive: My First Year of Teaching	135
21.	Edmonton County: The Best and Worst of Times	145
22.	Living Days	155
23.	Me and Mrs Jones	163
24.	What Lindy Did Next	169
	Postscript – Winning the Alternative Lottery	177

Chapter One

Emily Brontë and a Walk in the Woods

October 2011

•

Trent Park on the Outskirts of North London

The voice in my head is perfect. Well, not perfect in the way you might interpret that word, but perfect as in the way it used to be, before the neurons started to die off.

I'm walking in woodland with Scrappy, my Rescue Dog, a short-legged, scruffy, sandy-coloured mongrel. It's a cool autumn day and as I walk, I enjoy listening to my thoughts. I can say whole sentences, even paragraphs, each word flowing out effortlessly with no weird pronunciations or indistinguishable slur. In fact, if I don't speak out loud, it is possible for me to forget, for a few moments at least, that I am ill – seriously ill – as in incurably/fatally/terminally ill.

Outside in the open air, trees remind me that I am merely part of a world where living and dying are the natural order of things. One minute a fresh bud, the next a feeble, shrivelled leaf. That's the way it is and so the terror that grips me, almost all of the time now, can be momentarily soothed by the comforting sound of rustling leaves.

'Hey, Scraps, what are you doing?'

He turns from a pile of rotting dog-crap and wags his tail. I crunch determinedly across heaps of leaves and let my mind take me away. I become Emily Brontë roaming the moors, full of intensity, passion and suffering, plotting out my book, *Wuthering Heights*, as I soak in the wildness of dark skies over an inhospitable landscape. And then I'm Cathy, searching for my true love Heathcliff who I have so cruelly betrayed and lost.

As Scrappy fights his way through the brambles, the grass dissolves into wild purple heather, and whilst the leaves flutter down like orange snowflakes, I remember teaching *Wuthering*

Heights for A-level English. In those days, speaking was just something I did, non-stop, throughout the day, every day. Communication was my job; endless numbers of words rolled off my tongue without me giving any thought as to the importance of that muscle. I was, in fact, just like you before my tongue began to betray me.

Fanciful imaginings about the memoir I haven't even started are interrupted by Scrappy tearing off into what appears to be a lovely patch of grass, but instead is a stagnant pool of green slime. (A mistake I often made in my younger life with regard to men.)

'Scrappy, Scrappy!' I call, wondering if I will need to throw down the lead and dive in to rescue him. I'm not entirely convinced of his swimming skills, particularly with his thick, terrier fur. However, with a surprised expression on his face, he scrabbles towards the bank, thick black mud clinging to his fur like a skin, and shakes himself vigorously. I laugh, and jump away from him. Then, after rolling around in some dry leaves, he bounds off in pursuit of a small squirrel sitting brazenly at the base of a nearby tree trunk. How happy and carefree he is, I think with sudden sadness.

'Do you want to go in the woods?' I ask him after he's raced back. I look enviously at the huge, red tongue hanging out of his mouth, and think of the sad, floppy one in mine that stops me forming words.

We set off together towards a wooded area on our right.

Once again I am wild, rebellious Emily, striding through crisp leaves, ducking branches and wrestling with ideas and emotions; and once again I return to my unwritten memoir, trying out various poetic and gripping first sentences that will instantly draw a reader in. This one, of course, will definitely get published, unlike the other three manuscripts that sit forlornly on a shelf. No, this one will make me famous, not as a vacuous, talentless celebrity, but as the victim of a rare, neurological illness yet still 'Living Life to the Full', as they say in the world of popular magazines.

I imagine myself stylishly positioned against red velvet cushions on one of those chat shows about 'amazing people' (my speech having miraculously improved). Everyone watching the show, whilst admiring my bravery, wit and courage, weeps as I tell them about the neurologist who informed me that my illness would make my tongue shrivel up so that I'd talk like Donald Duck.

'What a woman,' they will say to each other, 'how courageous she is, still able to laugh and also to write such a fantastic book about this vicious and extremely rare disease.'

I gulp back a cold stab of terror. Now, thirteen months after diagnosis, it seems impossible to take it in that my life is coming to an end and that each passing day takes me nearer to my own vanishing.

But then, a sharp stinging. Something small and spiteful lands on my head and I am back in Trent Park.

Bloody acorns, I think, as I look around the familiar soggy mud and realise that I haven't a clue as to where I am, and have obviously (and typically) not been paying any attention to where I am going. However, confident that the car park can't be far off, I call to Scrappy, who has his head inside a hollow at the base of a tree and we set off in a different direction.

After about ten minutes I look around nervously. Where is everyone? Scrappy sniffs the air cautiously as I hover uncertainly by two paths. Which one to take? Then I notice a red-brick house peeking through a clump of dense trees. Since when did people live in the middle of Trent Park?

As we walk around in circles, I imagine the Blair Witch watching from inside that sweet little cottage. Suddenly, I feel childishly vulnerable and scared.

'Find Mum's car, Scrappy,' I tell him, without much hope. He cocks his head quizzically to one side then races over towards a grey squirrel nibbling on an acorn.

'Scraps, they bite. You won't like them.' I say as he continues to leap at the trunk.

But then, ah, civilisation. A sign: Middlesex University. A sigh of relief is quickly followed by the question of the car park – like where the fuck is it?

Scrappy pulls me enthusiastically along the road marked 'exit', but at least another twenty minutes have now passed.

A girl, well, young woman really, appears behind me, fiddling with her phone. She wears jeans and is carrying a folder and is most probably, I brilliantly conclude, a student. In my old life, I would have asked her where the road was leading me to, but not now. Not until I'm really desperate, I tell myself.

Aren't dogs supposed to have a sense of direction? However, 'home boy', as an order, has no effect on Scrappy as he proceeds to drag me, panting heavily, towards an old chicken bone. He grinds it noisily then swallows it in one, oblivious to my feeble cries of 'drop it', in case he starts to choke.

But then, yes! Oakwood tube station. Again, my appalling sense of direction somehow has been overcome.

As we turn into the road I spot a bus stop. Fantastic. Surely it can't be far back to Cockfosters? Scrappy loves going on buses, so when one finally arrives, we leap on nimbly. Two hardy pioneers, hot and tired from our long walk.

'I'm lost. I was walking in Trent Park, I need the Cockfosters Road, is it on this bus route?' I say to the bus conductor, forgetting about the weak, pink, flopping thing in my mouth that tries to pass itself off as a tongue. The way he stares at me, I might as well be the Blair Witch herself, because what he hears is more like: 'Ay ost I worring Tent park... I need copfosts oad...'

A shadow of fear passes across his face as he tries to make out what I am saying. I can see his baldhead shining anxiously behind the plate of glass.

''Ock fosters Tent park?' I repeat, as a thick rope of saliva seeps down my chin. But then, dear Lord, the old 'emotional lability'– a symptom of my illness – manifests itself. (Uncontrollable and inappropriate outbursts of laughing or crying.) In this instance it is wild, noisy laughter, which in seconds is going to spray spit and snot all over the glass.

'I not noter neron,' I try to explain through my spluttering nasal giggle.

Again, nothing. He looks around in a bewildered way as if there might be someone with me, someone who might possibly be able to translate these honking seal noises for him.

'What?'

'Oh gok ay carn't speak,' I mutter into his frightened eyes.

'You just get off wherever you want, love,' he reassures, turning anxiously towards the steering wheel.

Everyone on the bus is staring at me, and not in an admiring way.

I glance around, but they instantly look down.

'Oh, well, boy, soon be home,' I whisper as Scrappy licks my wrist, happily oblivious to my slurred speech. 'Bet they all think I'm pissed, eh?' He smiles his doggy smile and yawns.

An old Greek lady, who has been watching me carefully, decides to try and help. She explains very, very, slowly that Cockfosters is on the left after the next stop. 'You... get... off...'

'Thanks.' (That's an easy word). And she manages to smile back, albeit a little uncertainly, as if I might have a machete hidden in my shoulder bag.

Finally. Finally. Three hours after I've set out, I am back in the loving arms of Bluey, my Beetle.

Tired and preoccupied, I clamber into the back seat, next to Scrappy and, as I fiddle with his 'doggy safety belt', a blast of wind wrenches the passenger door open. The groan of metal squeaking against metal simply doesn't register with me at all.

'Oh, you are a good boy.' I rub my face on Scrappy's head and breathe in his comforting smell. His long, red tongue curls itself around my nose. (Note to myself: tell director to focus on this poignant little scene when book is made into film; a close-up of the dog's healthy tongue = symbolic message.)

'Don't you want your door back?'

A blonde head suddenly appears out of the window of the huge, shiny 4x4 parked next to me. Busy fiddling with the clips on Scrappy's harness, I haven't noticed it. As I heave myself up, I stare in horror at the way my blue door is pressed against hers. Oh God, oh God, oh God, please don't let it have marked her car. I pull it gently towards me. No damage, phew.

My faint little 'sowee' clearly makes her decide to rethink her next comment, but I seethe inside, hating the pathetic apology and my eagerness to accept the blame. (I suffer from Instant Guilt Syndrome.)

'Don't you know I'm fucking terminally ill?' I want to yell.

I switch the engine on.

And then, suddenly, my relief at being back safely in my dear little blue Beetle turns to rage.

Wild, wild, totally inappropriate rage.

' I 'on't ant ay door ack, I 'ont my seech!' I scream as loudly as I can at the steering wheel whilst switching the ignition on.

I press my foot hard on the accelerator and drive dramatically out of the car park into the pale dusky October evening. Only, the trouble is, I can't see a damn thing. All the frustration, the fury, the despair, erupts. Tears and slobber explode out over my face and cover the steering wheel.

Fuck it. Fuck my stupid, weak lips and useless tongue. I screech to a stop, shaking, my hands covered with slime.

I scrabble for a tissue and wipe down my face and chin. Scrappy is whimpering softly in the back seat.

I undo my safety belt and turn around as his head appears on my shoulder.

'It's all right, boy, I'm all right,' he pushes his nose against me and I feel his reassuring tongue warm my cheek.

Blowing my nose, I fast forward the CD to my favourite Amy Winehouse track 'Back to Black', turn the stereo up to volume nine and head left towards Southgate.

'We only said goodbye with words', seems, suddenly, like a strange message to me. I can no longer speak words clearly, but I can still write them.

That's what I'll do, then, I think, as I put the car into fourth gear.

I'll say goodbye with words.

Chapter Two

Appointments with Doctor Death

August/September 2010

•

In an 'angry fucking hell' kind of mood, when I want to wallow in a trough of self-pity, I get out my diary and add to the list of possible reasons as to how I lost my membership of the Good Health Club. So far I've managed ten, but there may well be more.

Unfortunately, no doctor or scientist so far has been able to explain why someone is afflicted so. In my case, my cherub-faced neurologist, at least twenty years younger than me, tried his hardest in the face of my hysterical outburst. But what else could he have said to my pleas of 'how and why'? Other than it was plain old, bad luck.

There is no way it was to do with poor diet: the family joke when I was growing up was that mum and dad could always tell where I'd been sitting, as there was always either an apple core or a banana skin nearby. My sister's nickname for me was 'fruit bat'. I didn't eat biscuits, crisps, burgers or takeaways. And what about the broccoli that Gareth used to tease me about? I'd eaten fields of the stuff to ward off illness. Yes, I'd had a good, healthy diet, despite a passionate on/off love affair with nicotine and white wine.

So here's the list, so far, of possible 'triggers' for my illness:

1. The Grim Reaper's little idea of fun to punish me for cracking a joke on the telephone when I made my appointment with a neurologist called Dr Mort.
2. Too much Sylvia Plath poetry.
3. An unhealthy interest in books about death and suicide.
4. An overactive imagination, possibly traced back to Mad Mary, my grandma, who had a lobotomy in the

1960s to cure her of the voices she heard, and her obsession with germs.

5. As a person who has always both feared and imagined the worst, I might have invited illness into my body: a sort of 'karma'.

6. Weak neurons which have been contaminated by a faulty gene, possibly number nine, have been festering away in some hidden place for years, gradually getting weaker and weaker.

7. Writing to someone on Death Row in America might have stimulated an unconscious death-wish.

8. A lifetime of 'living on my nerves', as my mum used to tell me I did, has worn them away.

9. A book on my dad's bookshelf in the family home called *The Wish To Fall Ill*. Hadn't I longed for something to happen to me so that I could escape the stress of the tough Tottenham school?'

10. The trauma of a false accusation of assault made against me in 2005.

I read somewhere that cancer patients are encouraged to try and visualise their cancer, and then to mentally zap it. So maybe if I could conjure up a few neurons, I might be able to reignite them with one of those weird clicking implements we used to have in the kitchen to light up the gas.

So far, the clearest image I have come up with is that of a dying firework spluttering feebly in a dark garden, railing against its short spectacular life.

However, fireworks aside, what I do know for certain is that these neurons send messages to the muscles, and once they've fizzled out, I'm afraid to tell you, it's all over. Messages terminate, muscles atrophy, and you are trapped in your own body with no way of moving, talking or eating. In other words, life as you knew it has gone.

Doctors talk to you in platitudes and nervous euphemisms about being positive and not catastrophising the end. But you both know that basically you are totally fucked.

•

Early Days
•

On an August afternoon in 2010, I was sitting in the hospital waiting-room of the neurology department in a North London suburb, flicking through magazines and drinking coffee, trying my hardest not to appear to be a patient. I was wearing a leopard-skin-printed dress and my favourite red sandals. My hair had been freshly highlighted and I might even have added a bit of red lipstick, so completely confident was I that when Dr Mort met me striding into his consulting rooms, he would immediately see that I was a fit and healthy person who was here by mistake. A mix-up of files most definitely would turn out to be the problem, or the trapped nerve my doctor brother, Viv, had suggested.

Instead, after shaking hands, introducing himself and exchanging pleasantries, this happened.

'You're slurring.' Dr Mort remarked assertively as I sat down.

'Yes, I know.' I was shocked and not a little uneasy that he had noticed so soon that something had changed about my speech. However, his youthful, freckled face and friendly manner in no way hinted at anything sinister. He smiled warmly.

'Now, Mrs Jones, can you move your tongue from side to side?'

'Of course,'' I replied, wondering what on earth that had to do with anything. Okay, so it had become a little sore in recent months and when going through my 'tongue-cancer stage', I had noticed that the sides were slightly jagged, as if a mouse had taken a few nibbles. But the Maxillofacial man had convinced me that I was biting my tongue at night because of stress, and that I definitely did not have any sign of cancer.

However, when I opened my mouth to show off the marvellous strength of my tongue, I became, suddenly and terribly aware that it moved at a very slow rate, rather like an elderly tortoise.

It was nothing like Dr Mort's tongue, which sped up and down behind his bottom lip with amazing speed.

'How about a whistle?'

This again was disappointing. My lips attempted one, but all that came out was a faint noise.

'I've never been much good at whistling,' I giggled, trying to add a note of flippancy to the serious atmosphere in the room.

'Mmmm, any weight loss?'

'I wish.' I said, emitting a great loud guffaw of laughter whilst patting my fat menopausal stomach.

He didn't respond.

'Do you often laugh?' he asked, reaching for a small tool with a bright light on its end. Was he now making judgments about my personality? Another awful desire to crack a joke about my incredible wit and sense of humour was, thankfully, crushed by the ensuing examination of my spine, legs, shoulders and arms. He hummed a bit and then asked in a worryingly serious voice: 'Is your husband with you?'

I was momentarily struck dumb. Did I look like the kind of pathetic woman who has to drag her husband around for everything? I am an independent, professional woman. I'd been Head of English for seven years for heaven's sake. Instead, a wobbling little voice asked:

'No, why?' This was definitely not sounding very comforting. Where was the 'nothing to worry about, Mrs Jones'. In *my* script that was the line he was supposed to say.

'I... 'em... need to do some more tests, to, 'em... rule out something.'

'Why? What do you suspect?' I blurted out.

'Well... I'm... I'd like to talk to both of you before I give you a proper diagnosis.'

'You have to say something, Doctor, about what you suspect, please.'

The anxious begging tone worked, but the answer was simply, unbelievable.

'I... I... 'em... just want to run some tests on you to rule out... 'em... Motor Neurone Disease.'

'MOTOR NEURONE DISEASE!' I screamed.

Wheelchair, choking, paralysis, death. I knew enough.

'What? I mean, how? I mean... I don't understand!'

I was crying now. A dreadful, dreadful thing had been unleashed inside me. Poor Dr Mort. He flinched awkwardly, probably already regretting his disclosure.

'I don't understand,' I squawked, 'I don't feel ill, it's... it's... just my speech.' Dr Mort nodded understandingly as he passed me a tissue.

'Does that mean I'm going to die?' I snorted, my voice straining in desperation.

'Mrs Jones, we're all going to die one day,' he said.

Fucking great. That didn't console me in the slightest. I didn't want some sort of crappy, philosophy lesson; I wanted to know what was going to happen to *me*, Lindy.

'We need to arrange some tests and I'll see you again on the second of September, but now I need to give your husband a quick call.' Dr Mort became very animated and efficient, relieved to have something to do as I sat blubbing while trying to remember Gareth's work number. I imagined him in his office, busy on his Apple Mac, Radio Two blaring out, totally oblivious to what was about to happen to him. He hadn't been worried about me at all, putting it all down to stress and exhaustion, not this.

I think at that point Dr Mort was trying to explain the tests, but I'm afraid to say I couldn't take in what a MUNE test was, though 'body scan' I knew meant lying inside a giant toilet-roll whilst trying not to have a panic attack in the claustrophobic space.

'Cheerio, then, Mrs Jones, try and enjoy your holiday, and I'll see you and your husband on September second.' It was as if we'd just agreed on some successful business transaction. 'Turn left, then right, to book the scan.'

How could I have treated this appointment so casually? How was it possible that I might be terminally ill? I am never sick, I've never even had the flu.

The nice lady at the scan place tried to reassure me it would probably be nothing.

I drove home in a tear-filled daze.

I'll tell you right now, going on the internet after a consultation with a neurologist is definitely not a good idea.

As soon as I reached home I literally raced upstairs to my laptop and googled 'Motor Neurone Disease'. Here is a brief summary of what I found:

- 50% of people die within 14 months of being diagnosed
- More men than women get it
- 5,000 people in the UK are affected
- The annual incidence of MND is two cases per 100,000 people
- The disease is very individual so no patient can be told how it will progress
- It can cause people to suffer from emotional lability, in other words, inappropriate laughter or crying (hence the questions about my laughter)
- Life expectancy is 2–5 years

From this information I worked out that I might be dead by next October. How I got through the next two weeks, I don't know. Everyday, the shadow of a fatal, degenerative illness framed each waking moment.

As I sobbed in his arms several times a day, Gareth would reassure me that whatever happened he would be there to support me.

The 1st of September 2010
·

This was going to be my second year at a challenging school in Tottenham and I had been really hoping it would be a bit easier than the first. Downshifting when you're in your fifties is not at all easy, and despite no longer being ground down by school data, performance management, staffing problems and examination results, I had found it very, very hard to follow the set schemes of work. And I missed having the power to do things my way.

So, there I was, back at work waiting for the 2nd of September to come, too terrified to talk in case anyone noticed there was something wrong with me. Sitting in my Year-group meeting and waiting for my turn to introduce myself was agony.

I mostly stayed away from everyone by hiding in my class-room, sorting out various things. There was no way I could join in with the 'how was your holiday?' kind of conversations that sprouted up when you met someone new.

Finally, I managed to say to my Head of Department, my friend, Eileen, 'I think I may be going to get some very bad news tomorrow about my health.'

We went to see the Head, who was kind and sympathetic and insisted I go home, trying to convince me that doctors didn't always get things right. Unfortunately, I didn't for a moment think that a neurologist would have ventured such a diagnosis without being pretty sure.

D–Day – The 2nd of September 2010
.

Neither Gareth nor I slept much that night. We were early for the nine o'clock appointment and wandered around the grounds, not daring to say anything to each other. It was one of those beautiful autumn mornings, the sun shimmering above the trees. Gareth put his arm round me as we headed for the neurology department.

At nine o'clock, Dr Mort came out of his office, gestured for us to follow him, and seconds later we were all shaking hands.

'Now,' he said, smoothing out the piles of paper on his posh, wooden desk, 'I have the results of the tests here.' He pointed at a collection of papers. We both nodded, staring, whilst Dr Mort shuffled through them.

'And I'm sorry to tell you, that it is what I suspected.' He didn't seem able to say the word.

'You mean I have got Motor Neurone Disease?'

'Hmm, yes, I'm afraid so, Mrs Jones, but there are new treatments being worked on all the time… now I need to get you back into the National Health Service. Marvellous hospital, The Royal Free… bla, bla, bla, bla…' I held Gareth's hand like I was never going to be able to let go of it. Dr Mort began typing things into a computer, then scribbling-down his own notes.

As he wrote, it was as if I were watching myself as a character in one of the novels I might have once taught. There I am, a frail, gaunt version of my former self, pale but still glamorous, asking in a wobbly, yet strong voice: How long have I got then, Doctor?

However, the reality was that I did not sound brave or noble, it was more of a terrified squawk stuttered out between sobs, and I was hardly a slender or tragic heroine.

His answer to that immortal and cheesy question: How long have I got? was this:

'It's hard to say exactly, probably two to five years.' Dr Mort seemed keen to finish this conversation because obviously there aren't many comforting words to say to someone when the big, fat, finger of death is pointing right at them.

Five years max then, takes me to sixty, if I'm lucky. What has happened to my German granny's peasant genes that got her to ninety-nine and her three remaining children into their eighties? And what about mum's side of the family, her death at sixty-nine was seen as young?

No one spoke.

And then, Dr Mort stood up briskly and smiled.

'Take care, Mrs Jones; nice to meet you, Mr Jones.' He opened the door and we shuffled towards it.

'Thank you,' we both said. Though for what I don't know. Thank you for telling us that I wasn't going to get better? Thank you for being so cheerful about it?

We walked in silence towards the car park in the bright autumn sun. How cruel to receive devastating news on such a lovely, innocent day. If this was a novel, it would definitely have been raining, and the doomed heroine would be dry-eyed with bravery, not sobbing uncontrollably into a sodden tissue the way I was.

As we drove home from the hospital, the role I had often cast for myself as tragic heroine did not materialise. Instead, sitting in the passenger seat of a bright green Ford Fiesta, I was merely a plump, middle-aged woman, already planning how I was going to do away with myself before I turned into a helpless, paralysed blob. All I could think about as we sped down Green Lanes was my unwillingness over the past few months to face up to symptoms which, like the trail of sweets in *Hansel and Gretel,* had been leading me straight towards the cottage in the woods where old Madam Blair Witch herself was rubbing her gnarled hands in excitement for my grand entrance.

From now onwards, the 2nd of September was to become 'The First Day of the Rest Of My Life'. The day from which I would measure and track my own inevitable decline.

Chapter Three

Inside the Blair Witch's Cottage

September 2010

•

From the beginning of 2010, I had a feeling of fragility – of not being able to cope with difficult students anymore. All my experience and expertise as a teacher had no effect on the classes in my new school. Each day I willed the hours to be over, knowing that at any moment there was a distinct possibility that something might happen that would precipitate me into my car, and I would drive home and never, ever, return. Career over.

Finally, the moment arrived. The seeds had been sown by a girl with 'anger issues'. In March, she and her little mates had been hitting Charlie on the head with a rolled up playscript I'd written for them. Despite promising to behave, 'Angry' become more and more manic and the lesson had reached the tipping point all teachers recognise, when control is about to be lost.

I had told her to give the paper to me, but as I reached out and held the end, she snatched it out of my hand, rolled it back into a tube, and lashed out at my neck. The shock, thankfully, stopped me from giving her a mouthful, but as I sent her out and phoned for a member of Senior Management, I burst into tears. Big Mistake.

For six months after that incident, I battled through every lesson, trying to make a breakthrough and win them over, but it was useless. I had always managed to win classes over before, but this Year-8 group were crazy and uncontrollable. I now felt that my power had gone. The kids were right, I couldn't control them. I was crap. Totally fucking useless.

Hunched up and weeping in the school office on that day of reckoning, all I could think of was running away. I'd never felt so utterly desperate.

'What's happened to you?' Eileen asked, as if she also knew, like I did, that something about me was different. Senior staff insisted I go home, worried by my hysterical sobbing. But for me the situation had become intolerable, because I knew my reactions over the past six months had marked me out as a victim, someone whom the kids could torment.

All spring and summer before my diagnosis, there had been strange, peculiar changes. The throat that felt sticky; the tongue that became sore; the jokey accusations from friends about being pissed. Then, one morning, waking up to discover dribble oozing from the left side of my mouth.

Sore tongue websites are seriously scary. Images of this small but powerful muscle in various stages of disintegration and deformity are definitely not recommended for viewing. But I couldn't keep away from them. Peering at mine in the mirror revealed a rather lumpy looking surface that, if I studied it carefully, appeared to be twitching.

Each day drew me back again to the site, hoping for some comforting little diagnosis, like a mouth ulcer. Once lessons were over, there I was guiltily hunched over my computer with a small hand-mirror beside me, googling through every possible diagnosis.

All through the summer term, my fear grew, like the way you make a snowball, rolling it over and over until it grows so large that you're crouched in its shadow.

'Does my tongue look weird?' I asked Gareth one evening. I might as well have asked him if I looked fat.

'No, Pindles, it's just a tongue,' he replied, turning back to the newspaper. He'd lived long enough with the spot/mole/eczema that might be cancer, or the terrible headaches which signified a brain tumour, to take any notice of my medical dramas, which he put down to watching too much *Casualty* (might have to add that to the list).

I thought about Dr Strom, the handsome Dutch doctor in our practice, telling me that he thought I might have had a stroke. Now, with the true assessment of my condition, a stroke or cancer would definitely have been preferable. At least, with those, there was a chance of a cure.

•

After leaving Dr Mort, Gareth and I rode towards home in an uneasy silence. 'What about the boys?' I finally managed to ask him we as turned into our road. 'How do we tell them?'

'We'll tell them together when Robbie's back on Sunday. You can't tell Owen before.' Gareth turned the engine off, he was crying.

'I can't believe this has happened to you, Pindles, it's so fucking unfair.' He reached out for my hand which was slimy with snot.

'Oh, God, sorry.' A half-sob, half-snort of laughter erupted. The whole scene was unreal. Gareth and I had just driven back from seeing a neurologist who'd told me I was terminally ill. *Me*? Surely I was going to wake up soon and return to my ordinary little life.

I don't remember what we did after we got home from the hospital on September 2nd, apart from cry. Well, I cried whilst Gareth tried to be strong telling by me that there was still time left to enjoy life. We had one horrible conversation about our plans for a new life outside London, realising that it would not now, ever happen.

There would be no ramshackle old cottage by the sea filled with dogs and excited grandchildren. No joining amateur dramatic groups and chatting the night away with bottles of wine and new friends. No writing my bestseller. It was all over. The future had been ripped from us whilst we were looking the other way.

'This can't be real,' I sobbed repeatedly that evening, knocking back glass after glass of wine, desperate to reach some sort of drunken oblivion. I woke up in the middle of the first night of my new life with my heart pounding, too frightened to sleep in case that when I woke up again I'd already be totally paralysed – a sad, wasted figure unable even to hold a pen.

That first day of the rest of my life was spent wandering from room to room crying, as if, in one of them, I might find an answer to explain what had happened to me. And how would I tell my two lovely boys that I was going to leave them? Each time I thought of their faces, I would break out in fresh howls of despair.

Who was I if I was no longer Lindy Jones, the teacher? Talking was my life, it's what I did. What would I do with myself day after day? Sit around snivelling whilst I waited for the inevitable shutting down of my muscles now that those neurons had decided to give up on me?

Dr Mort had not been able to give us any information about the disease because, basically, it affects everyone in a different way. However, as the muscles in my tongue had already been affected, speech and swallowing would probably, but not necessarily, deteriorate first. And, at some point in the future, I would no longer be able to talk or eat food. Food, no problem, I'd never been a foodie, but talking was a whole different matter. Talking was my life.

And then the question of telling the boys as well as the rest of the family and friends. How do we even start? The point was, I didn't appear to be ill, looked perfectly healthy, but even as I went about the normal business of life, those fucking neurons had gone on strike and there wasn't a damn thing anyone could do about it.

We waited two days until Robbie came back home to tell Owen and him. This is almost too painful to write about; I'm sure you can imagine the reaction of two young men just starting out in life trying to take in the news that their mum was now terminally ill.

The first few days after the diagnosis passed in a blur of numb disbelief. I don't think 'why me?' came into it as much as 'how?' Or are they the same question? But my main tortured thought was: Had I done this to myself with overwork? Had it been the last few years of pressure that had finally just worn me out? And how could someone like me now be officially dying?

Other than the 'how' question, what was I going to do with myself day after day on my own in the house with only morbid thoughts to keep me company?

Of course, there were cards, e-mails, phone calls, texts from friends, ex-pupils and family. Their shock always precipitating an urgent need to see me, to reassure themselves I was still alive. But once in the house my friends often floundered, searching hopelessly for something positive to say. But there were no comforting little phrases which could make me feel better. Whatever way you look at it, there is no spin you can put on being unable to speak, eat or walk.

Hours of total despair were intermittently broken up by strange times of normality. Tragic heroines did not go to Morrisons, or hang washing out; they looked pale and thin, stoically bearing their suffering. I, on the other hand, was still obese according to Robbie's electronic scales, and with a large, red nose made sore by all the loud snorting into tissues for hours at a time.

Flowers and get-well cards came from students at school with kind messages about what a great friend/inspirational teacher/wonderful woman I *had been*. Who was this person? Certainly not anyone I recognised. Truthfully, it was as if I had already snuffed it and was at my own funeral, hearing people vastly exaggerating my virtues. 'Had been' summed it up perfectly; I was now living in the past tense.

One friend came to see me and actually started studying the width of the rooms, mentally measuring up the house to see if a wheelchair would fit in – which, she informed me, it would. I'm sure she thought she was being supportive. Although her next comment about what a pity there was no euthanasia in the UK left me wordless and wishing we had a gas oven, so that she could gently rest my head on some freshly laundered tea-towels before switching it on.

Even worse were friends who came to visit and just chatted about their piles of schoolwork and their summer holiday weight gain. Surely, they realised that I was no longer part of their world. That I had, in a very short space of time, transformed from overworked teacher to the elephant in the room.

No one could comfort me, but my family tried their hardest.

'Mum, we're all scared,' Owen admitted one afternoon in response to my self-pitying sobs.

'We need you, Pindles,' Gareth told me frequently, his eyes filling with tears.

'Mum, you're not alone we're all in this,' Robbie would say bravely.

'Mum, I know I don't show it much, but I do love you,' Owen told me tearfully on one occasion.

The warmth of the words from my family and so many of my friends, gradually and slowly, began to drag me back from frequent melodramatic outbursts about killing myself. But that was before Scrappy came into our lives.

'I want a dog,' I slurred one evening, between sobs. My eight-year-old self had made a promise to a poor unloved dog of the future that one day I would go down to Battersea Dogs Home and bring it home. Now, I was no longer going to be working full time, it began to dawn on me that this was one thing I could do.

'Let's get one then,' Gareth said.

What, no argument?

'Do you mean it?' I asked. For the first time in weeks, I felt a stirring of something other than misery.

'Yeah, why not, it'll stop you lying in bed crying.' Gareth put his arm round me. 'I hate leaving you so upset every day.'

Some days I hadn't even made it out of my dressing gown or stopped crying for longer than ten minutes. But now, now I was energised. I could reclaim myself as a dog rescuer, already seeing myself with a dog like Greyfriars Bobby, who would be so loyal and devoted that he would howl inconsolably at my grave for years after my demise.

I began maniacally scanning the Battersea Dogs for Adoption pages, stopping to sob melodramatically every hour or so.

'A dog will come to you,' said my lovely osteopath, Fiona, a few days later.

And she was right.

But, oh boy, there were a few nasty surprises ahead.

Chapter Four

The Last Bite is the Deepest

September 2010

•

It's a warm Sunday afternoon in South London, an alien environment to us 'Norf Lunduners'. It feels weird and unsettling, as if we've gone abroad. The last time I was in Battersea was when I went to the funfair that used to be here some forty years ago.

We begin our tour of the Rescue Centre on the ground floor. The sound of barking is deafening and there are masses of people peering at the dogs and scribbling details down.

'Oh, look, Gareth.' Bertie, a small black-and-white mongrel in the first pen runs towards me from his bed, his stumpy tail wagging hopefully. 'He's sweet. Oh. Not cat friendly, what a shame.'

Gareth moves nervously away from the enormous Husky in the next pen whose shiny nose is pressed tightly against the wire.

'Jeez, this one's massive.' I hear a slight tremor of fear in his voice. Bluebell licks her lips and cocks her head. There is something very disconcerting about those pale blue eyes.

'Why would you have a Husky in London, they are supposed to be pulling sledges?' I think, as I give Bertie a regretful last look.

Pudsy is whining as we stop at her pen. She only has one eye, which is fixed desperately on us.

Freddy, a Doberman, lies on his bed with his back to everyone. I remember my mum talking about patients she had nursed who had simply given up and turned towards the wall.

I try calling his name, but he doesn't respond.

There are so many dogs here at Battersea Dogs Home pacing around, sadly asleep or barking loudly. It's like Death Row for dogs, row after row of condemned prisoners, victims of the human race.

Most of them are Staffies or bigger versions that are most probably mixed with Pit Bull terriers, so my dog expert friend, Sandy, has informed me. She explained that genuine Staffordshire terriers are quite small and not intrinsically vicious, but in my head they are in the same category as Rottweilers. Despite being told by a man in the park recently that Henrietta, of the drooling jaws, was just a big, soppy baby.

'It's not the dog anyway, it's how they've been treated,' Sandy said.

Wise words because, a bit like internet dating, you can never be exactly sure what you are told about them is the truth.

After our walk around, we are interviewed about our suitability as responsible doggy parents. When I got our two rescue cats, a thin serious-looking woman came to inspect the house. She wanted to see the garden and tutted a lot about the fact that the North Circular Road was so close. But this time, no mention of a home visit.

We pass our interview, and next weekend we can return to choose a dog. After the last few weeks of total unremitting misery, I am now going to have my own dog. A loyal, protective companion and friend.

I spent the rest of the following week on the Battersea website, taking notes about the new dogs up for adoption.

Every now and again I wail and sob to Gareth about whether this is a crazy idea altogether. Could I take a dog for a walk if I am in a wheelchair? But that's when denial comes in because, I have already decided, I'm never going to be in one.

'Look, you're fine at the moment, a dog will give you exercise. You could have one of those little scooter things.' Gareth picks up the *Evening Standard*.

'What, one of those fatmobiles?'

A vision of myself whizzing dramatically across the North Circular, hair and scarf blowing in the wind, is instantly replaced by the picture of the scooter, running over my beloved pet as it stops for a quick wee.

'My arms might be paralysed,' I sniff, scrolling down the photographs. I stop at Chico. 'You're not even listening.' I blow my nose. 'The cats won't like having a dog. Evie is purring happily in my lap, unaware, as I was before a few weeks ago, that her life is about to dramatically change.

'Well, they'll have to lump it, they are idiots. Fourteen years with us and they still run away from me,' Gareth offered.

'That's because you don't like them.' Evie rubs her face against my arm purring loudly.

'No, but I love dogs,' he says, launching into his anecdotes about Spot One and Spot Two, his loyal childhood friends. 'Look you want a dog don't you?'

'Yes.'

'Right then.'

'A dog will come to you,' Fiona Osteopath's words float back. It sounds all mystical and cosmic, as if somewhere out there is a poor unloved mongrel with a little label on him, waiting especially for me. A kind of doggy guardian-angel.

Euston, the following Saturday. My sister, Karey, is standing by Paperchase in her bright green coat, waving. She's come down from Derbyshire for the day to see me and help us choose a dog. We haven't seen each other since my diagnosis so there's a lot of hugging and crying.

Soon we are wandering around the corridors of dogs in their pens. Depression descends. Where are the ordinary mongrels – those quirky, scruffy little mutts that you used to see everywhere?

We then head for the viewing room where we sit and wait for a dog to be brought up. I am not at all hopeful that we are going to find one.

First, a little wiry terrier, Jack. He is the right size, friendly, but when a huge tabby cat is brought into the room inside a cat carrier he lunges at it, barking furiously. The cat hisses and spits, but when Jack returns for a second and third attempt to clamp his jaws round the enticing ball of fur, our blossoming relationship is over. He has failed the cat test.

Pickle, Mavis and Butch all behave in the same way. Things are not looking promising. Then I mention Scrappy, a small sandy-coloured terrier I have seen on the website, and minutes later he runs in wagging his tail and heads straight for my sister.

Karey throws a ball as they bring fat tabby cat back in.

Scrappy pounces once but is clearly frightened by the serious amount of hissing and growling emanating from this spitting fur ball. Looking rather spooked, he runs after the ball instead.

Gareth is already gushing about him and I notice that Scrappy could be his dog brother. They both have similar coloured hair, a beard and a slightly unkempt appearance. Scrappy's tail wags constantly and he is definitely more interested in the ball than fat cat, who is following his every move with bright green eyes.

Scrappy bounds towards me and licks my hand. His tail is waving around madly as he sniffs my legs. He has little tufty eyebrows and within seconds I have fallen. His 'love me' eyes are irresistible.

'Yes, yes, we'll have him,' I say. Beaming smiles of satisfaction all round. He isn't too big, tolerates cats and appears to adore everyone.

Later we meet up with my brother, Viv, in Covent Garden and celebrate Scrappy Day, and I realise I have managed for a few hours to forget that I am ill.

•

Now, every teacher knows that there is something called the 'honeymoon period' when you first meet a new class, particularly Year 7s, and they are still smart in their fresh new blazers and neat little ties. And believe me, even with years of experience, you can still be caught out. It really is possible to believe, in those early weeks, that you have finally met the 'dream team': the perfect class that will stay as their little perfect selves for the rest of the academic year.

Wrong.

As soon as this absurd thought is allowed in, you must crush it instantly underfoot, just the way that first cheeky bit of backchat must be acted on.

So, when Scrappy sank his teeth into my cleaning lady's leg three weeks later, we should have taken it as a warning, not plied poor Irene with Scrappy's anxiety issues and Rescue Dog insecurity by justifying how, when she brought a cup near to me, his damaged mind thought he needed to protect me.

'Bad boy,' I told him as he stared at Irene's chunky thighs, not appearing to be at all sorry. I kept apologising and then led him firmly into the back room.

'Irene, God, I'm so sorry,' was all I could think to say. Scrappy's bouncing happiness had already taken our minds off my illness, despite the fact he had forgotten that he had passed the Cat Test. Instead, he couldn't believe his luck. He had humans who fussed over him and real-life furry toys which ran around upstairs, peering daringly through the banisters as he barked maniacally by the stair gate we'd had to put up.

Irene was understanding, but it had unsettled me. The information from Battersea had not mentioned that he was aggressive, merely that he'd spent his earlier days with five other dogs rampaging around a house, crapping in the garden, fighting with his brothers and sisters and with no visits to the outside world.

The next day when I got the new ball-thrower thingy out of its packet, Scrappy cringed away from me, huddled in terror next to the tumble dryer. His ears were flattened against his head as if he expected a beating.

'Oh, Scraps, it's all right, Mum's not going to hit you.' A faint tremor of the tail. I let him sniff the ball thrower and he calmed down.

Since my diagnosis a lot of people had come to the house. Friends, my brother and sister, as well as various MND professionals. Scrappy had been delightful with them all, friendly, calm and happy lying by my feet on the floor whilst I bemoaned my fate. But, later that week, when my friend Noel popped in, the hug, and my crying triggered some loud growling and teeth baring. What was happening?

Then he started barking at white-haired old people with sticks, flashing his teeth at my disabled neighbour, which was so embarrassing.

'You need to get him neutered.' Sandy, my dog-expert friend, told me. 'And you should put him in dog-training classes.'

The honeymoon was over but what were we to do? Meanwhile, I was sinking into total despair.

The following week when Irene came, Scrappy barked at

her again. Unable to face the ensuing tension and explanation as to why I wasn't at work, I grabbed his lead and headed out. I hadn't even brushed my hair.

We headed for what we locals call 'dog shit alley', thinking it would be quiet. But no. I'd forgotten. At nine in the morning everyone is scurrying off to work. But not me. No. Never again. I'd never again be struggling into a staffroom with bags full of exercise books. I was finished. A nobody. My transfer to the 'sick world' complete.

I gasped back a pathetic sort of snorting sob. I was fumbling to tie a knot in a Morrison's bag full of Scrappy poo, when I heard a voice, a familiar one.

'Lindy? Is that you? Is that your dog? Aren't you at school?'

'No... no, I... I'm not well... I've been diagnosed with... with... Motor Neurone Disease.'

Lynne's eyes widened with disbelief as she struggled to speak.

'Oh, no, oh, God... fuck... I'm so sorry,' she said as she flung her arms round me unaware that a stinking Morrisons bag was inches from her smart, black jacket. 'Is he your dog?'

We both looked at Scrappy who was pressed in terror against the wire fence, eyeing up the two alien legs that were entwined with mine. I pulled back from her, instantly trying to explain that he was a Rescue Dog and a little 'unpredictable'.

'Oh... oh, God, oh, poor you.' The kind words set off a wild spluttering of tears. 'Look, I must dash but I'll ring you, right?'

'Yes, thanks.'

She turned to wave as I stuffed the bag of Scrappy's poo into the red box and it was only then that I realised I'd got one white and one black shoe on.

October came and by now Scrappy had also bitten dad's lady friend, Jenny. He flinched away from children, cowered by road signs and growled at anyone who came to the house.

He cringed when I took his brush out and whined every time I went upstairs to 'cat land', where Evie and Squeak now spent their days.

Yet each day, the misery of my diagnosis was taken away by Scrappy's complete joy in my company. Every afternoon, he ran maniacally after his ball in the park, his tail constantly wagging as if powered by some sort of electrical force. And, if I wanted a good cry, I could bury my face in his thick curly hair and comfort myself with his doggy smell. I was totally in love.

However, I now started to keep him on a lead when someone came round, nervously watching him for any signs of teeth baring. But one day, feeling a bit more confident, I wrongly assumed that just because my friend Jill and I had taken him out to the park together, he was her new best friend. No. Big Mistake. When she followed me into the kitchen bringing her coffee cup, he seized the moment to fling himself at her legs, biting first one thigh and then the other.

'Oh, God… Scrappy… no… oh… God, Jill, I'm so sorry.' I grabbed his collar as Jill's face scrunched up with pain and shock.

'Lindy, he's a Rescue Dog…it's… well they can be a bit territorial.' Jill was wincing with pain whilst I waited for those comforting words, 'I'm fine'.

'I'm so, so, sorry,' I spluttered as I ordered him in to the back room. I slammed the door shut and burst into tears.

'I think we'll have to take him back to Battersea, you know I can't cope with him as well as everything else.'

Jill nodded in agreement as she limped towards me.

There followed the most miserable lunch I've ever had. At the restaurant, I could not stop the sobs for long enough to eat anything. I'd got a horrible illness and now a dangerous dog. Life had, in a few weeks, turned into a fucking nightmare.

After Jill had gone, I returned home to find Scrappy's sad face pressed against the glass panel in the door. His tail began wagging before I'd even opened it.

There were no smiles or cuddles from me. Instead, I stared at him firmly with my arms crossed.

'BAD, BAD, BOY!' The happiness at seeing me disappeared as he slunk down onto the floor, his ears flat against his head. He stared at me with those heart-breaking brown eyes.

'Oh, Scrappy, why? You can't stay with us if you keep biting people. Jill's one of my closest friends. Bad Boy!' I raised my voice and he cringed away from me.

He gingerly put his head down next to my foot and trembled.

'We're going to have to send you back, boy.' I was sobbing now. Big, noisy, messy sobs. Strings of my drool soaked the top of his head as I sat down next to him on the rug.

Nervously, he edged closer to me and licked my hand. Then rested his head on my knee.

'Sorry, boy, I didn't mean to shout.' He wagged his tail.

'Do you know Mum's ill?' This time he raised his head and wiped his hot tongue across my cheek and when I laughed he sprang up and rolled onto his back, his tail thumping the floor with happiness.

'You don't like Mum crying, eh?' More wriggling and tail wagging.

He leapt up and raced to fetch my shoe from the sofa – throwing it into the air and then diving down to pick it up. Soon I was giggling and pretending that I was a dog too. It was impossible not to be infected by Scrappy's love of his new life.

I rubbed his neck breathing in his comforting smell, a reminder of my childhood with Perdy. There was no way I could possibly take him back to Battersea. Hadn't I decided I wanted to give love to an unwanted dog? What did I expect? Poor Scrappy. What effect had all my crying had on his poor, little, damaged dog brain?

'I think you need some therapy, Scraps.'

Chapter Five

Therapy

October 2010

•

Session One: Molly

•

A brown-eyed woman with thick, curly hair sits earnestly forward on our faded, velvet sofa. I'm on the edge of the black leather sofa, clutching a scrunched-up piece of tissue paper. I notice my bitten fingernails. She holds her slender, pale hands together, almost as if she is praying. However, she's not a nun, but a social worker from The North London Hospice that my kind doctor organised after my hysterical sobbing and wailing in the surgery the previous week. Terminally ill people are her speciality.

A similar age to Molly, possibly, but this is not a meeting of equals even though in another lifetime we might have been friends. She has a kind face and when she speaks, comforting words run smoothly, like melting chocolate, out of her mouth.

'Think of it as being a journey, Lindy,' soothes Molly, passing me a fresh tissue.

'But it isn't one I've chosen to go on,' I snort loudly as Scrappy pushes his wet nose against my ankle.

'I know, it's really difficult for you to accept, but... well, we're all on the journey, the difference is, that you are... well, a little nearer to your destination.' Molly fiddles with her ring and tucks her auburn hair back behind her ear. Destination? I feel like snarling, that's a nice way of putting it, but I don't, she is far too sweet.

'But talking is my life, was my life... I mean I'm a teacher... I communicate all day, well, I used to.' I burst into tears again. 'I don't have a place anymore, Molly. I don't know how to live.' She nods empathetically, and I blurt out, 'Oh, God, listen to me, so melodramatic.'

Molly laughs. I love the way her warm, brown eyes crinkle up and, just briefly, I am back being the person I once was, the Lindy who could always make fun of herself.

'Yes, and I can see what a lively, humorous, outgoing person you are,' she says.

'Was,' I correct, 'that was the old me.' I bend down to stroke Scrappy, who wags his tail gratefully.

'No, you are, Lindy, you still are.'

'I hate the word 'terminal'. I mean how can that word have anything to do with me?' Sobs engulf me again. Scrappy twitches anxiously, he's on a lead just in case he decides that Molly is a dangerous enemy.

'Try and think of it as life-limiting, you still have some living to do,' Molly smoothes out her orange-and-black skirt, patting at a crease with long, delicate fingers.

She has allotted me an hour, once a week, and as she glances at her watch I'm suddenly afraid of being on my own.

'I don't even know why I've got a dog now, and a crazy one at that,' I gabble. 'I mean is it sensible?'

'Well, you told me last week that it has always been your dream to get a dog from Battersea Dogs Home, anyway he's a sweety, and he adores you.'

'Yes, he's brilliant, except for the biting!' I laugh.

'Listen, Lindy, I really need to get going, I'll see you next Tuesday then, all right?'

I want to hug her, but don't. She's a professional, a counsellor, not a friend.

When the front door closes I start bawling again, burying my wet face in Scrappy's soft, doggy hair.

'How can this have happened to me, Scrappy? How?'

Session Two: Dog School
•

I now live in a constant state of fear, not just about what will happen to me as my illness progresses, but of what Scrappy will do next.

I wrench him away from people we meet in the street, their calves far too near teeth level for comfort. A man comes round the corner with an umbrella and Scrappy lunges towards him as if he might be about to plunge a lethal weapon into his small, furry body.

'I'm so sorry,' I gasp, as Scrappy barks again, 'he's a Rescue Dog.'

'Ah, yes, poor lad,' he says giving him a sympathetic glance.

A delicate Japanese woman walks towards me with some fluffy pedigree that Scrappy takes an instant dislike to. She is not so understanding.

'What's wrong with your dog?' she snaps, pulling at the pink lead attached to her yapping little fur ball.

'Rescue Dog, sorry.' I don't know how much more of this I can take.

I'm going to try dog training first so I enrol for a six-week course, quite confident that Scrappy will learn quickly. He understands, 'sit', and is clearly intelligent. I am the first one at the Scout hall and Richard introduces himself to me.

'Just take a seat with Scruffy.'

'Scrappy.' Hearing his name he pricks his ears up and looks suspiciously as Richard studies him.

'He's a Rescue Dog,' I explain, pulling him away from Richard's legs.

'Ahh,' he says in a knowing tone, as I sit down.

'Good boy, Scrappy, sit.' He wags his tail and obeys but the moment someone else enters the hall, his mood changes and faint growls begin at the back of his throat. Oh, fuck.

A tall grey-haired man walks towards me with a bouncy, black Labrador puppy. He moves a chair next to me and Scrappy goes nuts, barking, then shows a snarling mouth of sharp, white teeth.

The man reins in his dog and scuttles away, but each time a dog or person comes anywhere near us the same thing happens.

For the actual training we move into the naughty corner.

'No one go near that Rescue Dog, please!' orders Richard, as we lurk in disgrace near the cupboards at the front.

At the end of the hour Richard signals for me to wait behind.

'Em... Mrs Jones,' he says as Scrappy growls at him,' I don't think this is er... quite the place for Scruffy.'

'Scrappy.'

'Yes, well, Scrappy obviously has some problems. I shall pay you a home visit next week and we'll assess what the next step should be, though do get him neutered as soon as possible.'

'Yes, yes, I will, but Battersea advised us to let him settle in for a couple of months first.' I want to cry. I want to cry so badly I can't look at him.

'Hmmm, well, don't wait too long,' he mutters, 'I'll come over on Friday, all right?'

'Yeah, okay,'

The training is over and we've been banned from completing the course, like two badly behaved schoolchildren.

Session Three: The Dog Behaviourist Visits

•

Richard sits down on to the sofa opposite us deliberately ignoring Scrappy, a technique apparently used to assert dominance over a dog by behaving as if the canine in question isn't in charge. Scrappy, however, is staring at Richard, his ears sharply upright, already suspicious of this bearded intruder.

Richard places his plastic bag on the sofa and reassures Gareth and I that he is not only a trainer but also a behaviourist, and has worked with lots of difficult dogs. We explain about what has happened with Scrappy recently.

Richard tells us he is ready to start and stands up taking a step towards Scrappy.

'Scraps, no,' I pull on the lead in as tightly as I can as he jumps up at Richard barking loudly and aggressively.

Suddenly, the plastic bag is flying through the air landing with a loud clatter near Scrappy who looks at it with total confusion, then glares back at Richard.

'It's full of biscuit-tin lids.'

'Ahh,' we both say.

'It's to send a message that this behaviour is unacceptable. Er... Mrs Jones, could you pass the bag back please.'

Once again, Richard walks towards Scrappy who, once again flashes his teeth and barks, albeit slightly less loudly. Afterwards as Richard nods his head in a concerned manner, Scrappy fixes his eyes firmly on the carrier bag and snuggles more closely to my legs.

This is not going well because as Richard's hand reaches towards the bag, Scrappy glares at him as if he'd like to grab him off the sofa and rip him limb from limb.

'Quite frankly, Mr Jones, Mrs Jones, you've got a very difficult dog here. In all my years working with them, I would say Scruffy here would come in the top 10% of the most aggressive ones.'

'Scrappy,' I mumble.

'Yes, I'm sorry. Frankly, if I were you I'd get him straight back to Battersea before he attacks anyone else.'

Gareth has gone white, he twitches uncomfortably next to Richard on the sofa. 'He might improve if we get him neutered,' he mutters weakly.

'He might,' says Richard, with absolutely no conviction.

I hear the beginnings of that all too familiar throaty growl bubbling at the back of Scrappy's throat.

We see Richard to the door and once closed, I burst into tears.

Scrappy is now happy again. Off the lead, he wriggles on his back, wagging his tail, then runs out to fetch Foxy his favourite toy with the dreadful, loud squeaker.

'What are we going to do?' I slurp, wiping my wet chin. The thought of being without Scrappy is too much too bear.

'We'll get him neutered and give him six months,' Gareth says. 'I can't believe he's a dangerous dog, look at him.'

He looks up at both of us lovingly with his huge brown eyes.

'Scrappy,' I say, smiling as he leaps up to lick my nose, 'you're okay, aren't you?'

And do you know what? It worked. Eat your heart out, Mr Big-Wig Behaviour Expert. Scrappy is now a totally reformed character. Ball-less and with lots of tail wagging TLC, he cheerfully greets everyone who comes to the house. Such is the power of love (and surgery).

Session Four: A Trouble Shared
•

Helen and I are sitting in a local café with two cappuccinos which we sip carefully. I already have a huge mass of coffee-stained tissues piled untidily next to my cup. Helen is far less messy.

Like me, she has MND and her speech has been affected. We met at the local support group, which initially I refused to go to on the grounds that I did not want to sit in a room with a load of people in wheelchairs. This makes me sound awful. But it is true. So far my only symptom is slightly slurred speech, and I have no intention of being reminded of what the future might hold.

However, loneliness and despair about the rarity of my condition caused me to change my mind. On a damp November morning we arrived at the North London branch meeting. I went straight over to sit next to a petite, blonde woman whom Gay, the branch co-ordinator, had introduced to me as Helen. One of the first things Helen told me was that each morning she wakes up grateful to be alive and mobile. I was in awe. What a woman. What spirit. She was also the same age as me, which, all things considered, makes me feel somehow a little less alone.

At the meeting we exchanged e-mail addresses and now meet regularly for coffee. So here we are, on a cold, dark December afternoon at Costa Coffee in Southgate.

'At least we can read and walk,' she says. Helen and I have already discovered a shared love of books.

'But the thing I hate most though is the drooling, don't you?' I say, mopping my chin. My coat already has brown blobs of drying froth sprinkled on the collar.

She nods and reminds me of the story she had told me about when she was leading a conference, lost control of her lips, and spurted coffee out all over her papers, just weeks before she finally admitted that she could no longer cope at work. She had had symptoms for several years which, in a weird kind of way, cheers me up. Maybe I won't be, as the internet has chillingly informed me, one of the 50% of those with bulbar or pseudobulbar palsy who die within 14 months.

We both start giggling in our awkward, noisy 'Motor Neurone' way and a man looks over from behind his laptop.

'I read an article in the paper this week about life spans and apparently butterflies only live a few weeks – a month in fact,' I tell her.

'Really? Poor things.'

'Yeah.' I nod in agreement. All that time spent crawling about in the dirt as a caterpillar, to discover you don't have much time at all to dance about, flashing your beautiful wings to the world.

I don't know her well enough to know if she appreciates my sense of humour in saying this, so instead I go for the spiritual approach.

'So, basically, they have to make the most of each moment. That's what I try and do now. I mean... when I stand in the park watching Scrappy running towards me with his ball in his mouth... it just makes me feel... well... just grateful I'm still here.'

Helen nods knowingly. God, I feel so earnest and stoic for about two seconds before embarrassment sets in. I cringe at the way illness has changed me into someone who spews out repulsive little uplifting phrases whilst missing out the fact that I spend a lot of the time writhing around on the sofa at home incapacitated by terror and despair. I'm definitely more caterpillar than butterfly.

She smiles a sad smile.

'It's not fair though, is it?'

'No.'

Tears threaten to start, and I want to reach across the table and hug her.

' I know what you mean though and hey, whilst we're still butterflies, we'd better make the best of our gorgeousness, I mean before we...' Helen says.

There is a future we can't put words to – can't even bear to contemplate. But, before I can make a silly remark about turning into a caterpillar, Helen has a bad coughing fit.

I pat her on her back whilst watching a small, black mongrel cock his leg outside on the lamppost, then wag his tail as his owner speaks to him. Animals are lucky, I think, they don't know they are going to die. I want to say this, but death seems an inappropriate subject for two people, sitting in Costa Coffee who hardly know each other.

'I'm glad I've met you,' Helen says, 'I don't know anyone else with Motor Neurone, do you?'

'No.'

And in that instant, I realise again how the connection of being ill is so immensely comforting.

'Yeah, me too,' I say, 'glad we've met, I mean.'

And I am. Very, very glad.

Chapter Six

Trees, Leaves, and Peanut Butter Sandwiches

November 2011

•

Before becoming ill, I never really gave trees much thought. They were just there, so familiar to the landscape that there was no reason to look at them. Not anymore. Now every time I walk anywhere I study them, mapping out my illness in seasons. My second autumn with MND... second winter... second spring? The leaves aren't giving anything away.

Last week, in the local park, the shift into winter was nearly complete and the squirrels were out in force, taunting Scrappy with their tails as they ran up and down the tree trunks.

'Look, Scrap, up there, what is it?'

I love the effect that this excited voice always has on him: he instantly springs into squirrel mode, sniffing the air, ears pricked up with excitement. He barks loudly at the branches of the silver birch tree, perhaps hoping that one might fall into his jaws.

I follow his gaze, and then on up past the tops of the branches towards the blue of a November afternoon. The trees lean together making a sculpture with their branches, some still proudly showing off the last of their bright orange and yellow leaves.

This scene reminded me of a game that I used as a teacher, to introduce the concept of metaphor.

There were various categories; trees, fruits, animals; anything in fact. Students were encouraged to think about character rather than physical appearance, as there was always some little smart-arse who wanted to compare his mate with a plate of curry or a burger.

Kids, sorry, learners, as we must now refer to them, would then hopefully write something like, 'If I was a fruit I'd be a pineapple, hard on the outside but sweet beneath my skin.'

Trying to work out whether I'd be a banana or a peach, I noticed, just at eye level, a small crumpled leaf.

'Hey, Scraps, there I am… that's me,' I said, as I watched it clinging bravely onto the branch. Oh, yes, that was definitely me.

'If I was something in nature, I'd be the last autumn leaf left on the tree. Frail, but determined, not quite ready to let go of the branch. What do you reckon, Scrappy? Do you think Mum's clever?'

Scrappy cocked his head, panting heavily, a collection of rather papery leaves hanging from his beard. He wagged his tail and cocked his leg against a bush.

Strolling back to the car park, I have to confess I was quite impressed by the metaphor. I made a mental note to feed it into my book. Not that it really cheered me up. I was still reeling from the discussion with my speech therapist about having a PEG fitted.

'Come on, boy, this way,' I called as Scrappy proudly crouched down and discharged an enormous steaming dog-crap. I scooped it up, along with a few leaves. What a way to go. After all the blossom and brightness of the summer months, you end your life wrapped around a large turd in a Morrisons plastic bag. A metaphor to forget.

•

Yesterday, I was sitting in the hairdressers, and as Maria mixed a little pot of hair dye, a voice, which sounded vaguely familiar, turned into a face I couldn't possibly have forgotten.

'Miss Jones, hey, it's Paul.'

'Oh my God, Paul. Paul?' A bearded man is standing in front of me and is wrapping me in a huge bear hug.

'This is my favourite teacher,' he announces to everyone in the salon.

'How are you, Miss?'

And then, inevitably, reminded of my other life, I'm babbling and crying and trying to explain what has happened to turn me into the incoherent dribbler I now am, as opposed to the Head of English at Edmonton County School.

'You mean you've only got two weeks left to live?'

And then I'm laughing the way I used to when teaching Paul. I am back to my former life as Miss, the word I never hear anymore.

'No, no, years, maybe,' I splutter, sticking two fingers in the air.

'See what she's like,' Paul tells Maria, 'she's swearing at me now, like she used to. She was always sending me out, weren't you, Miss?'

Tears and giggles fight within me as Paul scribbles his mobile number down on my pad of special MND paper which says, 'I can understand you, but have difficulty speaking'.

'We'll meet for coffee in the New Year, have a proper catch up, yeah?'

'Great,' I nod.

Another massive hug follows.

'If there's anything I can do, ring me.' Maria is dabbing at her eyes, and I want to make a joke about this Oprah Winfrey moment, but as my witty remark will get lost in translation, I just nod my head and beam.

'Bye, see you in the New Year.' Paul waves to me from the door.

'We were in primary school together,' she tells me as she begins to smear the paste onto my hair. 'Such a nice boy.'

'Yes,' I whisper to my reflection, wanting to keep this feeling of being 'Miss' for a while longer. Visits to my previous healthy life still have the power to overwhelm me and as I watch my hair being swallowed up with goo, I'm back in the English office at Edmonton County. Someone professional and important.

'I bet you were a really good teacher, Lindy,'

'Yes, sometimes.' I laugh. My brief encounter with 'healthy self' has, despite it hurting, reminded me of how much, for the most of the time, I loved teaching.

Back at home, I opened the fridge and wondered what I could eat, now that it was all becoming such an effort. Despite finally getting to have the starring role in my own tragic novel, I was having a little trouble with the costume. Tragic heroines do not eat meals while wrapped up in old pillowcases, or tea towels, like some ridiculous mummy. Nor do they drool whenever they speak.

At this point I should explain the problems I have with eating and drinking so that you understand why social eating is no longer an enjoyable occasion.

Here they are then, in no particular order:

1. My tongue is weak, shrivelled and smaller which means it can't push the food around.
2. The muscle in my bottom lip is now so feeble that food and drink simply pour back out and over my chin.
3. The muscles controlling my swallowing are not very strong.
4. Liquid and food can miss the food pipe and go into my air pipe and lungs. This can cause choking or an infection.
5. Thin liquids like wine and water are hard to swallow.

Sometimes the whole process of puréeing, chewing, swallowing and slurping make eating such an effort it's easier not to bother. But unless I maintain a healthy weight, I will be down on PEG-lady's list of patients.

Last week I nearly choked to death in my own hallway whilst eating my lunch. It's hardly the stuff of tragedy, but that's the trouble with being in denial, sometimes it jumps out at you when you're not paying attention.

There I was, sitting at the kitchen table, reading e-mails. Not so much the 'elephant in the room' as the 'weirdo in the kitchen'. Scrappy was in his bed, next to the radiator, lying on his back as if he were sprawled out on a beach. I was wearing a green tea-towel round my neck as a bib and wrestling with special festive kitchen-roll every few seconds to mop my mouth.

Despite Robbie's warning about peanut butter, I could not resist it and had just crammed a wedge of thickly peanut-buttered bread into my mouth. This was not a great idea. Weakness in the tongue and mouth muscles mean serious problems with large pieces of un-chewed food, and already the wedge of sticky bread was rolling around at the top of my epiglottis.

Shit, God, oh, fuck. It's stuck. Breathe – can't breathe. Can't breathe.

Shout – can't. Fuck, fuck, fuck. Stand up. Quick. Bang on wall. YES. I'm slapping the wall with my hand. HELP ME! HELP ME!

'Mum, Mum!' Robbie has leapt out of the shower, thundered down the stairs and grabbed me under the ribs. Good old Heimlich Maneuver works. A piece of bread spews out of my throat onto the floor as I gasp for breath.

'Mum, Mum, you all right?'

Poor lad, he's draped in two towels and is soaking wet.

'Ye... Ye...' Breathing properly again is a miracle.

'I told you peanut butter was too sticky. Where's the bit that was stuck?'

Scrappy is cowering guiltily by the door, licking his lips.

'Oh, gross, did he eat it?'

I nod, helplessly gripped by the desire to both laugh and cry.

'I'm all right, honestly,' I finally manage to gasp.

•

It's strange isn't it, but if you'd said the word 'PEG' to me 18 months ago, I would have thought it referred to something you hang clothes out with, not some discreet little plastic tube that pumps nutritious formula into your stomach. Now the word is down there on the 'scary future list' along with breathing masks, wheelchairs, toilets that clean your bum whilst you sit on them, stair rails, lifts and light-writers.

Gloom has descended after an appointment with Gina, my speech therapist. Since the choking incident, eating has been harder. My hands have been feeling stiff. The tops of my arms are much weaker and I am sometimes breathless. Trying to comfort dad on the phone is almost impossible, so Gina has ordered me a light-writer, a machine that speaks typed words.

After 14 years together, dad's lady friend, Jenny, had told him she didn't feel well and needed to go and live with her daughter in Devon. Just like that. Within three weeks her house was on the market and she'd gone. Dad is heartbroken. Confused. And none of us know what to say. He was a psychoanalyst, so talking about things usually is second nature in our family.

'We didn't really discuss it,' he tells me every night on the phone, as he struggles to cope with the shock. No explanation other than 'I don't feel well' makes no sense from a woman who used to tell us regularly how she didn't feel her eighty years of age at all.

Tina came to deliver and to teach me how to use the lightwriter. It is small, but somewhat chunky, and unexpectedly heavy. When you type, letters appear on a screen and a voice is activated to speak out the words. I can't help laughing as Tina tells me to choose a voice. She advises against Rita, who sounds like she smokes about 50 fags a day, and Wendy, who obviously has had a sex change. We settle for Betty, though Rita sounds more my type – a bit wild and up for a laugh.

Soon, I'm typing in phrases I often use. 'Don't forget my Baileys with ice' and 'Have you fed the cats?' Scrappy runs in as I type his name, glaring suspiciously at the Christmas tree. Oh, and there's a doorbell noise for when I want attention. Hmm, sounds just what I need.

Later, I ring dad.

'It's so hard being on my own like this.' His voice crackles.

'I know, Dad, I feel so sorry for you.'

'What was that?

'I'm sorry that this has happened.'

'I didn't quite catch that, but it's lovely of you to phone.'

'Have you seen anyone today?'

'Sorry? Oh, you're a darling daughter.' His voice breaks.

'Lots of love, Dad.'

'Yes, you too.'

Scrappy licks my ear as I bury my face in his fur and cry.

Chapter Seven

Pollyanna has left the Building

December 2011

•

It's now been fifteen months since my diagnosis. Slowly, very slowly, I am reassembling myself. Not back in the saddle exactly, more like hopping around with one foot in the stirrup, cursing the gatecrashers who turned up to trash the celebrations of the festive season.

Accidents, illness and death have unfortunately been staying with us this Christmas, despite arriving without an invitation. I mean, wouldn't you think that a family coping with terminal illness as their permanent houseguest would have enough to contend with?

I am typing this on my beautiful MacAir, which, unfortunately has been a victim of one of these guests. Each day she plays little mind games with me as to whether she's going to turn on, ever since some idiot knocked a large glass of Baileys all over her.

According to Jeremy in the Apple Store, he's amazed she's still managing to switch on at all, as a quick peek under her silver case revealed a mass of crystallising fluids sticking to her precious parts.

'Once it's dried, well, I'm afraid that's it, Madam.' Jeremy frowned. 'It's not a good idea to have liquid near a computer.'

I glared at him, wishing I could make a scathing, sarcastic remark.

Robbie had received the short straw of taking me to the Apple Store in Brent Cross for a consultation. Judging from the way Jeremy directed all speech to him, he clearly thought that I was probably either an old lush or a bit simple. Possibly both.

'Please excuse my Mum, she's not well.'

I moved my lips to my ventriloquist-dummy smile, staying safely mysterious and drool-free.

51

'Thanks for your help,' said Rob to Jeremy as I packed the computer away.

'Mum, aren't you always telling us not to have a drink next to a computer?' he asked as we wove our way through crowds of frenzied people grabbing their bargains in the sales.

'I know, must be my illness.'

'Mum, you can't blame MND for everything.'

Something suddenly popped into my head from another lifetime ago. 'Hey, do you remember when you and O were little I told you that I'd I'd been listening to a programme about fear of insects and that if you gave them a name they became less scary.'

'William Wasp,' he laughed, 'yeah, I do.'

'So what name would you give MND then?' I asked.

'Mildred,' he announced as we reached the car.

'Hey, I like that. Mildred. It has a kind of bossy sound to it. Like someone who would walk into a room and start taking over.'

'You're crazy, Mum.'

'Do you know I never taught a girl called Mildred?' I mumbled, as he revved up. 'There was a Michael Michael and a Brad Pitt.'

'Mum, don't forget your computer might just crash one day, so just back everything up.'

•

It is the day before Christmas Eve. I have primed Betty with a few phrases, changed the sheets, hoovered the house and brought down the box of decorations. So far everything is going to plan. We have collected dad, made him supper and positioned him as near to the television as possible. I have put an extra table at the end of the sofa, which allows him to position his magnifying device, hearing-aid batteries and his glass of wine.

'You all right, Dad?' I help him to sit down, and rearrange the cushion he is struggling to tuck behind his back. I smooth down his hair and kiss his cheek.

'Phew, oh… oof, it's awful being old,' he mumbles.

'I know.' Though I don't. A childish little 'poor me' part

wants to remind him that I am never going to be, although by
the time Christmas is over I will have definitely changed my
mind about growing old and decrepit.

'I still don't understand why Jenny went to Devon.'

No, dad, none of us do. It's all he can think or talk about.

'You're a lovely daughter,' he whispers, his voice cracking.

Oh, dad. I hate being trapped by my speech. I let a few tears
silently trickle out.

The lights from the Christmas tree cast slithers of green and
red on the silver frame on the mantelpiece opposite. The Lucas
family, all five of us, poised for a moment in time, one summer
afternoon a long, long time ago. Dad is smiling and I am nestled
safely in his lap, but now his face is sad and whiskery. There
are little patches of silver hair that he hasn't been able to see
when shaving that make me want to cry.

'I'm sorry I'm so useless.' he says after a few more 'oofs' and
'phews'. He sinks back onto the scarlet cushion behind him.
'I still can't believe Jenny's in Devon,' he says, for about the
tenth time.

Distraction. That's what he needs.

'Hang on, Dad, I want to show you something.' I stand up
and lift heavy Betty off the table. I position her on my lap and
press the on button.

'What's that?' Dad peers closely at the blue machine that
resembles a small typewriter from the 1960s.

'It's called a light-writer.'

'A what?'

'It's to help me.'

I press another button. 'Have you fed the cats?' Oh, God,
wrong button. But, more worryingly, Betty seems to have been
visiting America since I last turned her on. Or maybe I hadn't
noticed her nasal Southern drawl before.

'What was that? Rats?' He turns as if looking for one.

'Sorry, Dad, wrong button, it's a machine to help me. I type
in words and it speaks them.'

I press Memo and W, for the phrases I've stored there.

'Would you like a glass of wine?' That's more like it, girl. Dad
stares suspiciously before letting his forefinger swoop down.

'Get me a Baileys and don't forget the ice,' Betty's imperious voice booms out.

'Dad, wait, let me press it, hang on.' I move his finger off the keyboard.

'What's it saying?'

I press again. 'Would you like a glass of wine?'

Had there ever been any female Daleks in *Doctor Who*? Because listening to Betty again, I feel sure she must have had a starring role as one. My hopes are fading.

'I can't understand it.' Dad slumps back against the cushions and sighs.

'Listen, Dad.'

I press memo and W again. For fucks' sake Betty, get it together.

'Would you like a glass of wine?'

'No... sorry... I...' Failure.

Betty is lucky I haven't hurled her across the room.

'Oh, I hate being old,' he says, shutting his eyes.

'Any chance of a top-up?' He holds out his empty wine glass. I manage to suppress a loud scream.

I pour myself a Baileys and quietly we sip our drinks together. I still have the framed picture next to me. It is the only one I've ever seen of us all together and I discovered it in amongst the hundreds of dad's photographs.

'Do you know where this photo was taken?'

'No idea. Hampstead Heath?' he mumbles, staring at it through his powerful magnifying glass. 'I'm eighty-five, you know.'

I might as well have shown him a load of strangers.

In the picture, mum's arms are almost thinner than baby Karey's legs. She's wearing a pink-and-black-spotted dress and looks amazingly glamorous considering she has an eight-month-old baby. Mum's 'best eater' – my little sister – sits awkwardly on her lap, whilst my brother, Viv, is held by an arm from each of them. I am leaning back in dad's arms, which are protectively wrapped around me. Daddy always made me feel safe, always calm, in a way that my volatile mother didn't. I was never scared of daddy.

Dad shuts his eyes and reaches for my hand, he is having one of his turns – some weird kind of epilepsy that makes him confused and incoherent.

'Oh, ah, oh.' He grips my hand more tightly. Oh, dad. My determined efforts to be jolly stop as I watch him close his eyes. All I can think about is flinging myself into his arms to be soothed and made better, back to being young again with my wonderful kind daddy. A noisy sob erupts as the door opens and Scrappy snuffles in, his nose focused on the carpet for bits of leftover food.

'Hello, boy.' He wags his tail and sniffs the air. Ah ha, he's detected the bit of custard on dad's trousers. Out curls his long, red tongue and within seconds he has wolfed down not only the blob of custard, but also a piece of fruitcake lodged on the side of dad's slippers. His nose detects the Baileys, which like my Mac, he has taken rather a liking to and he manoeuvres himself next to my glass.

'Av a dar.' Dad is staring around the sitting room as if seeing it for the first time. 'Fas ee bar...' The words swirl around in his mouth.

'It's all right, Dad, you're just having one of your thingies.' I stroke his warm, liver-spotted hand. I don't panic anymore, you just have to wait for them to pass, they last only a few minutes.

Meanwhile, I lift up the photograph and think about the man I'd once called 'daddy'. Christopher James Lucas, youngest son of Katarina Engelhart and Harold Lucas. He must have been doing his analytic training when this photograph was taken. Already a doctor, married to the beautiful red-haired nurse, Sheila Barcroft, who, although smiling brightly, is already in the full throws of the post-natal mental illness that shadowed my childhood.

I shut my eyes and remember.

Dad made up stories about a naughty elf called 'Trixie Gnome' who was always getting into trouble. He had such a calm comforting voice and I was a bad sleeper. It is easy to imagine mum, bad tempered and snappy, sending him in to try and induce sleep in her annoying daughter.

Along with Trixie, he also made up little relaxing scenes. 'You are lying on a raft… the water is lapping gently around you…'

'But, Daddy, there might be a shark.'

'No, no, just a calm sea. You are getting very, very tired now, your legs are heavy… and listen, the sleep fairies are here…' This was the moment when daddy made little fluttering noises, which were meant to be fairy wings. Even now, all these years later, I can still recall the feel of their feathery touch on my eyelids as I drifted off to sleep.

•

On Christmas Eve we receive news that Jenny, his lady friend, has had a stroke. I spend the afternoon with dad trying to console him. His sad, confused face is almost too much to bear.

We have a few people over for drinks in the evening. Jenny sounds in a fragile state, according to her family. Most of my friends know dad, so they have little chats with him whilst he tells each one the same story.

Christmas Day morning. I'm in the kitchen making toast for dad when I hear.

'You are fucking joking?'

Husband Gareth, a.k.a. the Welsh Dragon, has exploded. The eyes, I know, will be dangerously rolling around. Oh, God, what now? His temper is notorious and firmly blamed by us on his heritage and red hair. I know he's talking to Robbie because Rob has kindly given up his bed for Grandpa and is on the sofa in the front room. The dragon's voice cracks with rage as I strain to hear what has happened.

'You've lost your iPhone? I don't believe it!' This is shouted so loudly that Scrappy looks at me anxiously.

Oh, God, no. No, no, no, no. Not the beautiful iPhone 4 he's just bought.

'Have you a spot of marmalade?' Dad is holding a can of dog food up to his 'good eye'.

'Dad, that's dog food.'

'Someone in a mood?'

Yeah, you could say, I think as I unscrew the lid of the marmalade jar.

If the beloved phone has been lost, this is the end of any hope that the day might be salvaged.

'I can't believe it's Christmas Day,' dad says, as Scrappy hovers by his chair hoping for some delicious little morsel to fall his way.

'Hang on, Dad,'

'What's that?'

Here we go. Hello, 'special day', another 12 hours of trying to make myself understood. I head down the hall.

Rob is groaning on the sofa. Gareth has stomped off upstairs.

'It's true then, you've lost your new iPhone?'

'Yes, Mum. Don't go on, I know it's my fault. I shouldn't drink.'

If talking wasn't such an effort I might have reminded him of our discussions on the sensible drinking routine, but one glance at his face warns me off. Instead, I focus on the small pool of sick on the edge of the sheepskin rug and emit a loud pissed off sort of sigh.

'I know, Mum. You'd better see Owen, we... we... had a bit of a fight...'

'A fight? For God's sake!' They are twenty-two and twenty-four. 'I'd better go and see if he's all right.'

Upstairs, a body moans noisily from underneath a purple duvet. On one side of the hump is Evie, our small black cat, and mewing noisily by the pillow is Squeak, possibly the most annoying cat in the whole world. There's a pile of cat shit on the carpet, which I have to step over.

'Owen?'

'It's my knee... oh, my knee...' More muffled swear words and groaning emanate from underneath the duvet.

'He pushed me over, oh, oh, fuck, fuck, it hurts Mum.'

Painkillers and a packet of frozen peas are brought to him.

'I was telling him to calm down, Mum, like a phone is only a thing.' I know instantly what he means. Despite their outward bravado, Mildred impacts on them everyday; my deteriorating speech is a constant reminder that they are going to lose me.

'I'm sure it'll be all right, O.' I ruffle his hair while Squeak tries to bury himself under the duvet.

•

The lunch has been booked for twelve o'clock. We have found a walking stick for Owen. What a sight we look. Dad tottering unsteadily across the car park, Owen limping, his face pinched with pain, and everyone else in a mood. I can't help myself, emotional lability rises up inside me, and I start laughing.

'Mum, it's not funny,' Robbie says, but then breaks out into giggles. No one else is finding this amusing.

Owen is in so much pain, he can barely eat. Luckily, dad is oblivious to everything. I send a text to Robbie's phone begging whoever has taken it to hand it back as it was a gift from his terminally-ill mother.

My puréed meal arrives.

'That looks like dog poo,' Robbie says, and he and I are off laughing again. 'I'm still drunk you know,' he says.

'I wish I was,' Gareth grunts. He's got 'the face' on, despite hoovering succulent pieces of turkey into his mouth.

'Yeah, don't we all,' I snap, taking a spoonful of gravy-coloured goo.

'What?'

'Nusing.'

The pile of serviettes is growing around me as I mop my chin after each mouthful. I catch the eye of a woman looking at me.

'Any cranberry sauce?' dad asks. At least his appetite is un-affected.

'Jon has your phone,' Owen says to Robbie, 'you gave it to him last night.'

Oh, wow, oh, thank you, thank you, thank you, God.

'You can get it later,' Owen tells him, scrunching up his face. 'Oh, fuck, my knee.'

The meal is rushed through as Owen has turned worryingly pale, and now we finally realise that he is genuinely in agony. Unlike Robbie and myself, who moan loudly about minor ailments, Owen is a true stoic. In the evening I drive him to A&E, which results in the diagnosis of a torn ligament.

Robbie by now is wracked with guilt and can't do enough to make up for it. Promises of PC games are made as he squeezes into his horsehair shirt, a favourite joke we share about playing the suffering martyr. It's a role we have perfected that must always begin with the immortal phrase 'I'm fine', muttered through clenched teeth.

I promise Owen that in years to come he'll be able to call all sorts of favours from his brother by saying, 'Remember that Christmas…'

'Er, aren't I the one who's ill?' I mumble, as we bundle Owen, doped up on strong painkillers into the car.

'You're just looking after everyone, Mum. Ahhh…' he moans, trying to position his leg in the front seat.

I pick up his crutches and squeeze into the driving seat, making Grandpa 'ooofs' and 'phews'.

Robbie starts laughing. 'Hey, Mum, how many times do you think Grandpa has told us he's eighty-five?'

Owen groans gently. 'I never want to be old,' he mutters, before falling asleep.

Happy Christmas, everyone.

Chapter Eight

The PEG Lady

February 2012

•

It's a dark, winter morning. Heavy clouds carpet the sky and leafless trees stand huddled in corners next to the shabby buildings of Chase Farm Hospital.

I don't want to be here. I don't want to be a patient. And I really, really, don't want to have a PEG fitted.

In the freezing cold waiting room, I listen to two people complaining that they can't eat certain foods. They both look at me as if I might want to join in, but I get out my iPhone instead. Before Mildred, I was one of those people who loved to chat. Toilet queues, waiting rooms, train journeys... but now, anxiety about my speech keeps me silent.

'Mum, do you have to tell everyone your life story?' one of the boys might have said if we were out together. But I just couldn't help myself. I loved talking. Still do.

'Mrs Jones?' A brisk sounding, blonde woman calls my name and I follow her into a cramped office. We shake hands.

'You've been referred by Speech and Language. Do you understand what a PEG is?' She smoothes out a pile of papers and picks up a pen.

'Yes.' Instantly, tears bubble up. It's always the same. In a medical setting there's no hiding from illness. No pretending that I got here by mistake.

Nancy explains the procedure and assures me I won't find it too uncomfortable. Hmmm. The medical profession have coded euphemisms. 'Slightly sharp' means extremely painful, I had recently discovered.

I mostly nod and snivel, watching Nancy's mouth and lips forming words. What a miracle. I'm in awe. Lots and lots of sentences pour effortlessly out. Why hadn't I appreciated my own voice before?

She passes me a tissue and begins to explain what will happen when I come in.

On the day of the procedure they are going to thread a camera on a tube down my throat, which will head for my stomach. Like a worm, the tube will emerge through a small incision in my midriff, where it will rest gently under a cover until it's time to plug it in to a feeding pump.

The thought of a tube going down my throat causes instant panic until Nancy explains that I'll be given a drug to relax me.

'No one will know it's there,' she says, as she shuffles through a folder on her desk.

I imagine saying to people, 'you'll never guess what I've got.' Then flashing a bit of tube at them. As if.

'Yesh.' I nod, my mouth full of saliva. The word comes out as if I'm underwater.

'It will stop you worrying about eating... make sure you keep well-nourished. You know you are now at high risk of getting a chest infection, don't you?' Nancy puts her pen down, we both smell toast coming from somewhere.

'I... I... know.' I now usually end up coughing whenever I attempt to eat. I'm only supposed to have puréed meals, but every now and again I disregard these orders and try and attempt, maybe, cake, or bread and butter. But it's no good. Imagining is not the same as being able to persuade my tongue that it still has enough strength to push the food past my windpipe.

Sausages and mash, lasagne, pizza, peanut-butter sandwiches. All are now in the past – things I will never eat again, yet I can't help torturing myself by staring at people wolfing down huge plates of food. How casually they eat, not realising what a miracle the human body is and how agonising it is for me to watch them.

'Are you all right, Mrs Jones? I know this is very hard for you.' Nancy is studying me closely.

'Yesh, it makes my illness more real.' I talk very slowly, forming the words as carefully as I can. Has she understood me?

'I'm Jake the Peg, deedle-iddle-iddle-um.' Oh, no. Rolf Harris. An annoyingly stupid song from years ago has popped into my head.

'I understand. But you do definitely want a PEG? I mean, not everyone has one.' She links her fingers together under her chin and waits.

'Yesh.'

But I don't, not really. I mean who would? I don't want to be hooked up to a machine at night. I don't want to be reminded of my dying neurons each time I go to bed. But I do want to live, therefore I have to find a way to accept that the PEG is not an enemy, but a support. It's all about the way you think about something, so the self-help books tell you.

The muscles in the top of my arms start twitching. Mildred. Her sharp nails are scratching through the tissue, wearing the muscles away. Relentlessly. Day after day, her red nails clawing at me. Laughing.

In the early days I imagined insects, scuttling under my skin. I'd roll my sleeve up and watch, fascinated as the flesh flickered and twitched.

'Mrs Jones, are you all right?' I'm back, my ridiculous mind crashing into reality. An overactive imagination has always been my downfall, and now, trapped in my head, it seems to be getting more extreme.

'Yesh.'

'Right then, you'll be hearing from us soon with a date.' Nancy stands up and holds her hand out. 'Try not to worry.' Like everyone I've met in the Palliative Care team she's kind and understanding. It's not her fault I have MND.

I stumble towards the carpark and realise I have forgotten to get a ticket. So, after finding an official, I use my acting skills to explain that I haven't got one. I can just about say the words, 'no ticket'. This has the desired effect. The man trots off and I do my 'simple dummy smile' to the other guy, who nods vaguely. I flash my little card, which explains that I have a physical condition that affects my speech. He nods again. Maybe he can't read?

'HERE... IS.... YOUR... TICKET.' The other one speaks very slowly to me whilst I wonder if I've got the remains of the supplement food all over my chin.

On the drive home I think of all the questions I wanted to

ask about living with the PEG. As opposed to having it inserted. Will it stand permanently by the side of the bed like a sentry? Will I be able to use it?

I let myself in, expecting to be greeted by the happy face of Scrappy, who has learnt that people behind the door as the key turns will be someone he knows. But no little bouncing ball of scruffy hair. Weird. Where is he? Did I leave the back door open? Has he finally managed to leap over the fence at the end of the garden? I fling my keys and bag on the floor and rush into the kitchen. No. The back room. No. And then, barking.

'Scrappy? Where are you?'

I stand at the bottom of the stairs. From this angle you can see the cat flap put into the door of what was once my workroom. The cats can go out via an open window onto a roof and I can lock them in at night.

A big black nose and hairy beard are peering out of the cat flap which has been jammed open. The door is shut.

'Scrappy, what are you doing in here?' Which is of course rhetorical because I know exactly why he's been there. Food. His ever-sniffing nose has recently tracked down the enticing smell of fish-flavoured Morrison's pouches.

As I go upstairs I can hear him whining, tail in full throttle, thumping against the chest of drawers.

'Scraps?' The cat flap was twisted at an angle where he had obviously been trying to squeeze his stocky little body out. By now I am laughing so much that the plan to immerse myself in self-pity about the PEG has completely gone.

Scrappy is beside himself with joy, leaping up and down. There are no cats to be seen, but their bowls are empty, spotless. Not a blob of cat food left anywhere. Empty packets are scattered all over the floor, evidence that Scrappy has licked them thoroughly for every last slither.

He leaps on me, his fishy breath overpowering.

'Scraps, you're not meant to be up here.' But I'm not really cross, how can I be, when everyday he does something that takes my mind away from the future. This keeps me anchored in the present.

Later on I watch the news which is full of suffering and violence. The world seems chaotic, unstable. Death is everywhere as Syria sinks deeper into civil war. It makes what is happening to me, in the grand scheme of things, barely relevant. Illness and accidents happen all the time.

'God, Mum, the news is so depressing.' Robbie is back from work and is slumped on the sofa. I'm snuggled up on the other one, which I now call my 'nest' as it's piled high with expensive cushions from my favourite trendy shop in Muswell Hill.

I make a mental list of the blessings that mum was always telling me to count, and there are plenty.

If anything happened to one of my sons, now that would be far, far worse than MND.

'Fancy watching an episode of *Come Dine With Me*?' I ask.

I can't eat and Robbie is hardly a devotee of 'haute cuisine' but we love the sarcastic voiceover as various crazies attempt to convince the other people that their cooking is the best.

Scrappy yawns and snuggles down on his end of our sofa. He licks my toes then rolls onto his back.

On the tele, someone called Krista appears with her poodles, Ping and Pong, who have seats to eat with her at the table. She's going to make snail soup for her starter.

'Oh, gross,' mumbles Robbie.

Simple pleasures.

A window of contentment along the journey.

Chapter Nine

Dear Body

•

Tuesday March 13, 2012

Dear Body,

Bad news I'm afraid.

This time tomorrow you will be in hospital. This is because the muscles in your mouth and throat don't work properly anymore, and if you don't have medical help you and I will starve to death.

You will have a plastic tube with a camera put down your throat, which will then snake through you and pop out of a small incision made in your stomach wall. Liquid food can then be fed straight into you so you won't have to worry about things getting stuck or, worse, going into your windpipe.

I know, it sounds awful doesn't it? I'm scared too, but I've been told that they give you lots of drugs to help.

This is what is known as a PEG, not a clothes peg, but a 'percutaneous endoscopic gastrostomy'. Something that I never, ever, in our old life together imagined happening because you have always been so reliable and healthy.

Please try not to be too upset, it means that we can live together for a little bit longer, even though we can't eat real food. We should have celebrated our last meal together but, like so many last things, I didn't recognise the occasion at the time.

Body, I just wanted to tell you how sorry I am, that I didn't appreciate you enough when you were healthy. I was always complaining about your fat stomach, depriving you of food in a lifetime's attempt to stay slim. How I wish that instead of eating cottage cheese on Ryvitas every lunchtime, I had allowed you to have big chunky peanut-butter-and-banana sandwiches, washed down by sweet coffee and a piece of cake.

What a selfish cow I was, leaving you hungry for so much of the time.

What I'm trying to tell you, Body, is that I should have loved you more. Should have realised what a truly amazing machine you are, marvelled at the way everything worked so perfectly together. Now, each move, each step you allow me to take is precious because, one day, Body, I know you are going to give up on me. Motor Neurone Disease, which, like an uninvited guest, barged in to our lives 18 months ago, is going be the death of us, if you will pardon the expression.

I know. I am sad, too. I miss your voice. I miss the person you allowed me to be, but we had some good times together, didn't we? Some great boozy nights out, laughing with friends. I'm just really sorry that maybe I didn't care for you enough, cherish your beautiful curves and strong arms and legs. So, dearest Body, this is my way of marking the last day of our PEG-free life, only, before I go, can I ask a favour? Please try and keep the muscles in your chest strong. I've noticed recently, that you have started to become a little breathless, and it's scaring me. Please, please, give me another couple of years. Three would do, though five would be better, but I know that's unlikely. I have already had two. Please fight your hardest, because one is definitely not enough.

Don't cry, I know this is hard for you but we'll just have to learn to live with PEG. I mean, it's not as if we have any choice, do we?

Body, thank you for all the years of good health you have given me, and good luck for tomorrow.

Your friend and partner,
Lindy

Chapter Ten

Medical Procedures

March 2012

•

In my previous life as a healthy person, my highly-strung personality was often focused on the knowledge that a terrible catastrophe could, and probably would, occur at any time.

The spot by my eye would be a rare melanoma; a son not answering his phone meant a fatal stabbing. Catastrophe was always close, lurking by my side. A malevolent understudy watching out very, very carefully for the moment when it could stride out from the darkness and take centre stage.

Several years ago on a family holiday to Canada, my teenage sons persuaded me to go white water rafting. Despite obvious horrific scenes unfolding in my head of them both being swept to their deaths, I agreed. I really wanted them to be proud of me and show them that I could, *Feel the Fear and Do it Anyway*, in the words of Susan Jeffers.

To put this into context, earlier in the week I had failed to walk across a flimsy rope-bridge swaying high, far too high in fact, across a rocky canyon where tiny trees shimmered about a million feet below. Despite a promising first step, after a mistaken glance down, the terror became so overwhelming that I knew there was no way I was going to be able to cross it. The three alpha males who had marched to the other side without a backward glance were clutching their sides with laughter.

But now I again had the opportunity to prove myself. The frightened fawn (Gareth's frequent description of me) was no more. In her place was now a roaring lioness.

However, dressed in my black wetsuit I looked more like a portly penguin. And, at the end of the safety drill, I had this sudden urge to ask if anyone ever fell in.

The handsome young French guy who was going to be in

69

charge of our dinghy reassured me that it was very rare. (Just like MND.) But rarity does not stop something happening. Halfway down the second rapid, I found myself flying through air into the frothy water. There wasn't even time for the blood-curdling screams I had littered my teenage horror stories with. I was under, then up. Bobbing up and down, spitting and gasping as I remembered being told that you should reach out for the rope around the dinghy and try not to dangle your legs down in case they got stuck in a rock.

'Mum, Mum!' The next minute, Robbie was heaving me back on, hooking his hands under the straps of my life jacket as instructed so that the arms are not wrenched from their sockets.

'Oh, God, oh, bloody hell,' I spluttered as Gareth and Owen attempted to haul me into a sitting position.

So you see, as far as I was concerned it was not if, but when, the 'dreadful thing' would happen.

I was known in my first family as the Lucas who was always, 'boiling hot', 'dying for a drink' or 'bursting for the loo'. Moderation was not even in my vocabulary. Dad, a Freudian psychoanalyst who used words like neurotic and anxious, scared the shit out of my school friends with his pale blue eyes. Me, my sister and mum all fitted into the category of being 'highly strung'. Moods, temper tantrums and depression flowed in and out of us. But so did hysterical giggling.

It was a perfect set-up for dad. Undergoing his analytic training, he soon realised that he had his own personal group of neurotic women on which he could practise his psychological theories.

His analysis of my fear of wasps was, he concluded, to do with fearing the angry part of my own personality. I found this very annoying. Wasps, in my opinion, were simply nasty, yellow buzzing things whose sole function was to eat as much sweet stuff as they could before stinging you.

Freud's *Interpretation of Dreams*, one of twelve volumes on psycho dad's bookshelf, was another source of worry. I borrowed it after recording my dreams for a few weeks and was horrified to discover that anything shaped like a tree trunk or a pencil could be linked to a penis. Maybe I was going to morph into a sex maniac? Or worse, become a nympho, as my friends and I referred to ourselves if we fancied a boy.

Dad and my brother, Viv, were quieter, calmer, altogether a different breed, seeming to inherit sensible German genes from granny (dad's mother), who'd never even had a headache and spent her eighties and nineties playing her left hand versus her right hand at Scrabble.

•

Back in the present, a siren screams in the distance. A car door slams. My neighbour's African parrots sing through the walls and a noisy bluebottle buzzes around my head. The washing machine gurgles in the kitchen as Scrappy rushes out barking at the squirrels he imagines are waiting to play catch with him in the garden. Illness, accidents and death seem unimaginable in such a peaceful domestic setting. Sunshine lights up the dust and dog hair, as early blossoms float down from the trees and I pause from writing to pat Scrappy's head.

Last Wednesday, I went in to hospital to have the PEG put in. The nurses who had visited me earlier in the week were sweet, practical and had left an information booklet, which I had ignored. Its cover was a bizarre black-and-white photocopy of cheery, smiling faces. I mean why? Why would you beam so cheerfully at this prospect? Or worse still, did the designers of this leaflet have no idea what a PEG was?

In a novel there are clues carefully thrown in by the writer about what is going to unfold. But, as we grudgingly stuffed money into the hospital car park ticket machine last Wednesday, there were none. No single magpies or sudden dramatic changes in the weather. No encounters with strange men in dark clothes, just a moan to each other about the cheek of making patients pay to park, and how cold it was.

The walk to the Surgi-Centre gave us no indication that I was about to be the star in my own episode of *Casualty*, but as I sat in a poky office snivelling in a hospital gown, I sensed the first flickering of terror.

I was still wearing my knee-length boots, which the nurse had said I could keep on, but I felt ridiculous. Wrong. I fumbled tearfully with the ties. 'Designed by a man,' Delores the nurse told me as she took over.

'Why you crying? You be out in 20 minutes, no problem. Procedure simple. You remember nothing.' She passed me another tissue.

'They give you sedation, yes? You won't remember anything. Little camera down, whoops, all over.' She patted my shoulder as I noticed the splashes of mud and dribble all over my boots.

I climbed tearfully onto the trolley and waved at Gareth.

A room full of busy medical professionals. What am I doing here? How can I be a patient? The tears started up again. What a fucking crybaby.

'Don't you know who I am?' I wanted to scream.

'Now, Mrs Jones, try and relax.' Nancy, the PEG nurse, whispered as someone came towards me holding a syringe. Okay. I might have made that bit up because I can't really remember the details, Delores was right about that. But I was aware of something black and rubbery going into my mouth.

And then I was under, or out, or somewhere, when, in the darkness, something happened.

I was fighting against a wall. A room. A place without air. Something. Diving down. Hurting. What? No. No, Jesus, I'm dying. I really am. Speeding up again. Tightness. The darkness pressing against my throat. No. No. Help me, I was going. This was what dying felt like. No white lights and peaceful drifting, this was sheer terror in its hardest form.

And then, the room began to come back. Shapes formed, light returned. A face. Mum? Had I passed over into the dead zone?

A blonde head hovered over me. Hazy. Flickering in and out.

'Mrs Jones.'

'I'm not dead?' I managed to say.

'No, of course not. We don't let people die here.' Nancy patted my arm.

From somewhere came the urge to shout, 'I'm alive!' But I didn't. My throat was sore and my feet were cold. What had happened to my boots? Also, it was 10.30. One hour and 15 minutes had passed.

About half an hour later, I was lolling weakly on the trolley when I felt the back of my throat gargle. I coughed awkwardly. Clammy bubbles of mucus like a thick muddy torrent sealed up my windpipe and my next breath would not come.

I gasped again. And again and again. Nothing. There was no space for air. It felt as if someone's hands were round my throat.

Mildred.

She was here, right next to me, her long, bony fingers wrapped tightly round my neck and she was going to kill me.

I started to scream. Tearing at the neck of the gown.

'Can't...' And then I was thrashing about like some crazy fish, flinging my arms at the nurses around me.

'Try and keep calm, Mrs Jones.'

Calm? I'm fucking choking to death here. Calm? Do something!

By now I was trying to crawl down the trolley on my hands and knees, trying to rip my gown off. Help me help me, God, God, God, God. It was the peanut butter. That was it. Still stuck there, gluing my windpipe together. 'Help meeeeeeeeee!'

Rushing. Holding me down. An oxygen mask descended and someone injected something into my arm. Breathing. Yes. Yes.

The plastic dome hissed air back inside me.

A breath. How precious. And another.

'Try and relax now.' Confident voices. Calming. They weren't going to let me die. An X-ray. A senior consultant swept into the room.

'I can see the fluid here.' Two doctors were poring over the picture of my lungs.

Later on and still alive, a voice near me.

'You kept us on our toes this morning,' smiled a nurse as they wheeled me out of the room. It was two-thirty. Had I fallen asleep?

'Hey, how are you?' Gareth looked pale and confused. 'They kept saying you'd be out soon.'

I could only roll my eyes and fumble for his hand.

'They're taking you to the respiratory ward. You've got a chest infection. Pneumonia. They want to keep you in for a few days.'

So much for Delores' prediction.

I clutched hold of my oxygen mask as I was wheeled into an ambulance.

Gareth gave me the thumbs up as the doors shut.

'We're taking you to Cambridge ward, right love?'

Great. Thank God it wasn't Neurology, full of people unable to move or talk. Relief washed over me. I was safe. Hah!

Chapter Eleven

The Patient

March 2012

•

I arrive onto the ward a few minutes later, the youngest inmate by far. The oxygen mask is still attached to my face and I'm told I must keep it on for another 24 hours. My right arm is hooked up to a drip full of antibiotics and I feel like I've been kicked in the stomach by a horse. Gareth is tense. I watch him flick uneasy glances around the ward. I know how much he hates hospitals.

'I better go back and see Scrappy.'

I nod feebly.

'I'll be back tonight, okay?'

More nods.

As soon as Gareth is out of sight, I begin to focus on my surroundings. I manage to shuffle up to a semi-sitting position and gradually become aware of the other women in the ward.

'I haven't slept for three nights you know, dear, three nights,' the woman on my right repeats as a nurse appears.

'Now, come on, Rose, let's be giving you your medicine now.' Brisk, super fast and thorough, the blonde nurse hands her a tiny plastic beaker then reaches towards the file attached to the end of the bed. She writes quickly, glancing at her watch to check the time.

'But Kitty, I haven't slept for three nights.' Kitty's hands, like little claws, scamper backwards and forwards over the sheet.

'Now, now, Rose, come on,' she reprimands in a broad Irish accent, taking back the beaker and writing in the file again before she heads off towards the woman opposite me.

'Mary, Mary. Have you been coughing onto the bed? Oh lord. Connie, Connie,' she calls, 'she's been after spittin' her phlegm out onto the sheets, give us a hand would you, we need to change her.'

Almost engulfed by a huge mass of fluffy white hair, Mary lies holding the oxygen mask to her face.

'Mary, Mary, now look you can't be doing this, it's not hygienic.'

Mary's chest bubbles and explodes into a cough as Connie quickly draws the curtains round.

'Oh, dear, oh, dear, I can't stand it.' Rose is staring at the group huddled around the bed opposite her. They look like guests left over from *My Big Fat Gypsy Wedding*. The four women all wear enormous gold hoops in their ears and gabble away to the dark haired one in the bed, who periodically wheezes and splutters.

'Jesus wept, ya won't be goin' out for a fag now, Moira. Ya need to give them up.' The fat one, in tight, leopard-skin-print leggings, pats Moira's arm as she rummages around in her gold handbag, eventually pulling out a bright pink phone. I am fascinated at the way her red-and-silver thumbnail flies over the keyboard; such effortless grace and speed.

'Sheev, you comin' or what?' she barks at the one with a tight blonde ponytail. I wonder how Fatty ever managed to get into her leggings. 'Sheev' bends down to pick up her bag, exposing a huge red-and-black tattoo. Rose can't keep her eyes off it, pressing herself into her pillows as if, at any moment, they might all turn, teeth bared, and rip her into pieces.

A loud explosion of music blasts into the air.

'I'M IN THE 'OSPITAL, BABE.' The skinny one with black hair bellows into her phone as she totters out of the ward in her white-and-gold leather boots to continue the phone call. There's a sign up saying 'Two visitors only'. But the nurses ignore it; they are too busy and probably don't want a row.

The rest of the women, a gaggle of brightly coloured birds, gather round Moira. They wrap their sunbed-tanned arms around her, then head out of the ward. An uneasy peace descends. Until:

'Oh, oh... I can't stand it... I really can't.' Rose shuts her eyes, pulling the sheet right up to her chin. And then I notice the dark-haired woman in a chair next to Mary, who is starting to take off her clothes.

'Should I get the sausages out?' She shouts as she wrestles with her jumper. Once off, she begins on the next layer. Shit, should I do something? But I can't move or speak clearly. The blouse gone, the bra is pulled down. A huge, brown bosom flops pitifully out of it. Oh, God, God, God, thank God I'm never going to be old, I think, as she gets unsteadily to her feet.

Kitty has emerged from behind Mary's curtain and I start waving and pointing at the woman who is now completely topless and tottering around unsteadily by her bed. Any second now she's going to crash face down onto the floor.

'Prudence, Prudence, now where do you think you're goin'?' Kitty has noticed her now, acknowledging my gesture by smiling gratefully.

'Have you got my sausages?' she asks Kitty, as her poor body is squeezed back into its clothes.

'Prudence love, Prudence, you're in hospital, remember?' Quickly and efficiently re-clothed, Prudence sits and stares around her. Once Kitty is out of sight, she begins to undress herself again.

Despite the dull, thudding of the pain in my stomach, I have a peculiar sensation of joy inside me that I am still alive. Compared to these women, I am agile, mentally alert and young. My euphoria is cut short by an orderly asking me if I'd like a drink. Yes, please, a sweet latte I long to say, but he sees the 'nil by mouth' sign and moves onto Prudence. He plonks a tea down carelessly on her little table and moves on to Mary. There is no effort to help. Prudence reaches a shaking hand out towards her cup and I wait for it to spill, but she can't even reach the handle. It's too painful to watch her arm shaking, so I shut my eyes and try and block out the noise, but it's hopeless.

'Nurse, nurse, nurse,' cries the woman to the right of me. It's the first time I've heard her voice.

'Nurse, nurse, nurse, nurse.' The cry goes on and on. Why doesn't anyone come?

The nurses are not cruel or heartless, they just don't have time to sit and chat or put a hand out to comfort someone, though they try their best when they are not filling out patients' forms.

'I am a name, not a number,' the guy in the 60's TV programme, *The Prisoner*, used to say; now I know how he felt.
Like my dad, I'm no longer a professional. I have become a
number in the NHS, a faceless patient marooned in 'sickland'.
And it depresses the hell out of me.

'Don't you know who I am?' One of my dear young deputies,
five-foot bubbly Louise would ask naughty Year 7s she en-
countered messing about in the corridors.

In a huge school such as Edmonton County, invariably the
answer was a trembling 'no'.

Breathing deeply she would take a step towards them and
say in her most theatrical voice, 'Well ... *I'm* Mrs Derbyshire,
so you'd better stop messing around'. And then she'd sweep
off up the corridor leaving them open mouthed, as if they had
just had a close encounter with The Queen. Ahh, Louise and
Lindsay, my dear deputies, what lovely people, what brilliant
teachers...

I must have dozed off because when I open my eyes the sun
is out and for the first time I realise that from the ward you
can see a tree rich in pink blossom. And people. Lots of people,
all scurrying around like ants – in and out of buildings, along
paths, past the window. It's amazing to think that outside the
world is just going along without us in the same way it will
when we die, I think morbidly, as I look around sadly at the
other women. Luckily, reflections on mortality are interrupted
by an urgent need to pee, which could be tricky given the state
I am in.

'Umm, I...' I wave at a nurse I haven't seen before. She looks
irritated.

'Yes?'

'Pee,' I manage to say after removing the oxygen mask for a
second.

'You want bedpan?' I suppose I do, so I nod my head.

Seconds later I'm cocooned behind the curtains trying to
heave myself onto a circular cardboard object. I squirm and
struggle to get into the right position, but nothing happens.
Not even a trickle. All the waterfalls and gushing rivers I conjure up have no effect.

'Have you finished?' the nurse asks minutes later. She has dark-blonde hair scraped back into a French pleat, and a tense, angry expression etched onto a face that might, with a smile, be very pretty.

'No, I...'

'You said you wanted bedpan, yes? Don't ask, if you don't need.' A hand flashes out to snatch it away.

'Mrs Jones, you need to co-operate,' she snaps, and I snort out a horrible, inappropriate laugh. This doesn't go down well.

'You think funny?'

I want to explain that this is a symptom of my illness, that I can't help it, that the unkempt, laughing creature she can see has been taken over by a cruel body snatcher called 'Mildred'. She probably assumes I am either crazy, like poor old Prudence, or deliberately bloody-minded. Doesn't she know who I am?

'I stand... can't...' There is simply no way I can do a wee lying on my back like some helpless beetle.

'You want commode?'

'Yes.'

'You stand?' I could. God, what will happen if I can't? Her dark eyebrows move more closely together, twitching with irritation.

I nod as she pulls away the empty bedpan.

But getting up is harder than I thought and the nurses are not allowed to heave you around in case of back injury – theirs, not yours. So I begin the agonising process of moving myself, thinking all the time about poor old Gregor Samsa in *Metamorphosis*, waking up and finding himself transformed into an enormous insect. I tip sideways and my head flops down and wedges next to the bedside cabinet.

Wriggling and writhing like crazy, I eventually manage to stand. Finally, the beetle has landed. Unsteady legs wobble to support me.

Hurrah, see, I can do it. I can. I wish I could shout.

The commode arrives and Katya seems shocked that I have managed this feat. She gives me an admiring look and then, surprisingly, she guides me onto it.

Slumping back against the pillows, my earlier euphoria starts to evaporate. Gareth arrives with my phone charger.

'Hi, I got you some trashy magazines that you wanted.' He plonks them down on the table. 'It's taken me bloody hours to get here, M25 totally jammed, so's the A10. You okay?' He looks tired and strained.

I nod and put my thumb up. He doesn't stay long as communicating is almost impossible. My iPad needs charging and we have no paper.

After he's gone, I wish I had asked for some toothpaste and slippers. I shut my eyes, tired now when... A voice.

'And here in this bed we have Mrs Jones. She has Motor Neurone and aspirated during the procedure to insert a PEG, she is on antibiotics.'

A group of solemn-faced nurses stare at me and scribble onto their clipboards. No one smiles. No one acknowledges that I am even alive. I feel like one of those specimens you see in museums, a small, dead insect pinned by its wings onto a display board.

They move off as one. A scary collective mass, gliding menacingly around the ward, hovering like vultures by each bed. These are, of course, 'the night staff'.

When mum returned to nursing in the 1980s, she told me that those working at night were now mostly agency nurses, displaying none of the caring qualities that had been instilled during her training in the 1950s. She had been deeply shocked by their indifference.

Apart from having my children, I had never been a patient in a hospital before, but one look at those nurses is enough to warn me about unnecessary bell-ringing.

Despite Rose's declarations that she never sleeps, she snores loudly while I lie restlessly watching the clock, wide awake with pain and unable to operate my bed head.

'Time for your meds, Mrs Jones.' A short, smiling, black woman fiddles with my hand and puts another gleaming pack of liquid onto the stand.

It is 5.30 a.m. and I am fuddled and uncomfortable. The PEG site throbs whenever I try to move.

'Breakfast time.' A tall, red-haired guy stands in the middle of the room with a trolley full of toast and porridge. He hovers by my bed, the smell torture. It's months since I have been able to eat toast. A wave of self-pity washes through my rumbling stomach as he reads my 'nil by mouth' sign. I have not had any nourishment for about 36 hours. Water in a drip, yes, but that is all. I am starving and my lips are so dry and cracked I can barely move them.

And so the hours drag on. It is now Thursday but I could have been here all my life. By midday I find myself simply staring around the ward the way the other women do.

Moira is being moved. Soon her bed is wheeled off and another, neatly made up, is put in its place. 'Oh, thank God, thank God,' mumbles Rose.

Then, even more excitement when a group of medical students enter the ward. Fresh-faced and eager, they listen attentively whilst the doctor in charge gives out information about each of us. Soon, they are at my bed. Again, the ridiculous desire rises in me to tell them that my brother is a consultant; that I was Head of English; that I'm not really a patient.

'This is Rosalind Jones, who has Motor Neurone Disease. Referred from the surgi ward after aspirating during a PEG procedure.'

The older man with curly grey hair says. 'Bla bla bla bla...' Nod, scribble, nod, scribble. No one looks up. Am I fucking invisible as well as sick?

I can't even summon up my 'dummy smile', they all seem far too earnest. I turn my head away.

Sometime later, one of these eager beings, a short, jolly, brown-haired guy, actually walks across to me, smiles, and asks: 'Would you mind if my colleague could practise inserting a cannula into your veins?' I think back to the five attempts it took one doctor in the drug-trial unit, but the personal attention is undeniably flattering.

'Ummm, well, I don't have very good veins, but...' He has warm, puppy-dog eyes. 'Oh, well, all right then.' I am patting myself mentally for being such a sweet accommodating person when a dark-haired girl in a figure-clinging dress and high heels bounces over. She looks like she has just leapt off the catwalk. Jesus, is she a doctor?

As she puts her latex gloves on and raises up the needle, peering closely at its slender body, 'smiler' makes eye contact and in that split second manages to communicate to me her incompetence. Fuck, I've done it now, I think as I wait for the sharp scratch.

The pain as the needle strikes is unbearable. I bite my lip as she tries three more times, finally giving up.

'Your veins are not easy, sorry.' She flicks back her sleek, black hair. There is blood all over my hand, on the bedspread and on the floor, and I am trying desperately not to cry. She makes a cursory attempt to clean my hand, then disappears.

'Really sorry, she's not very good at them yet,' smiler says. I wish I could snap back a cutting comment about not having volunteered to act as a pincushion, but I nod my head in agreement, glancing down at my bloodstained fingers as he rushes off.

'What has been going on here?' Kitty is back on duty, furious at the mess left behind by the student. She instantly whips off the bedspread. 'Those doctors, can't even be bothered to clean up, eh?'

Drama over, the time drags on. I wonder what the PEG looks like and how I'll ever adjust to having one. Every few hours a nurse flushes it with water, attaching a syringe to the end of what resembles a transparent tyre-tube. I can barely bring myself to watch. The place where it has been inserted into me is covered with a dressing. I wonder what lies beneath. Depression settles over me.

By the time Gareth arrives, I have sunk deep into total despair. Poor man. He holds my hand as I wail, face down on the fresh bed cover.

'Everything all right?' It's Connie, the kind nurse who had brought me some hospital slippers earlier, then jokingly told me I had been flashing my backside at the men's ward as I toddled off to the toilet.

She puts her hand on my shoulder as I shudder and gasp with sobs. 'I woth … a … eacher, not … not … thith…' I point at myself.

'She was a teacher,' translates Gareth. I gesture wildly for my iPad.

'Head of English,' I tap spraying it with goblets of spit. I flop hopelessly back onto the bed. Connie smiles.

'I can see you as a teacher... really.'

I know she's just trying to be nice. She rubs my back. How am I ever going to adjust?

'There, there, Rosalind, you'll be going home soon.'

I cannot be comforted. This is not how my life was meant to be.

Gareth holds my hand and waits for the sobs to subside.

On Saturday morning a young, curly-haired male doctor arrives by my bed. I recognise him from the procedure room.

'Just popping in to see you, Mrs Jones. You gave us quite a scare on Wednesday.' He smiles warmly as he fumbles with his folder of notes.

'Oh,' I manage to mutter, wanting to ask him what exactly he means.

'You can go home today, that's fine, you're all right now.'

Later, in July, I have an appointment with Nancy to review my PEG and I ask her if I had nearly died.

'Yes... yes, you did... your body went into shock because of your respiratory weakness.'

Fucking hell, I think as I stumble out into the bright sunshine, I knew it. So, I tell myself, you're in your second life now, girl, imagine if you'd popped your clogs back in March. Wow. Think of what I would have missed. And for a few minutes I actually experience an unfamiliar emotion: happiness.

Chapter Twelve

The Dying Line

April 2012

•

An unseasonably warm March has given way to a bitterly cold spring. Daffodils huddle sadly in the park, their yellow heads pointed towards the grass. I know how they feel.

I look at the trees. Some have a few tentative early buds, whilst others shiver in bright blossom, already appearing to regret their early burst of life. I am freezing. I look tiny in my white puffa coat. Like I'm wrapped up in a giant marshmallow. The bony shoulders I used to long for now make me sad, not pleased. Poor body.

Head down, lost in morbid thoughts of my own death, I am not paying attention to anything. So I don't notice the grey-bearded man in a bulky raincoat looming towards me, until he stops on the path and points in Scrappy's direction.

Scrappy is busy crapping over some daffodils, his whiskery face tense with concentration. I know, without having to feel, that my pockets are empty. The two bargain poopy-bags Gareth bought from the Pound Shop have already been used up. Damn.

'Oh, dear,' I mumble, fumbling in my pockets. My speech has alarmed him and he is peering suspiciously at me from beneath his bushy eyebrows, hesitating for about two seconds before he thrusts a crumpled Morrisons bag into my hand.

'Thanks,' I say in my weird nasal voice.

He studies me closely as if thinking of saying something, and then sets off down the path whilst I scuttle back towards Scrappy and the offending deposit.

The grass is long and I can't see it anywhere. Scrappy stands watching me diffidently as I circle around the daffodils.

'Where's your poo, Scrap?' He cocks one ear and wags his tail. I glance over at the man as if to prove to him that I am a caring dog-owner.

But now he's with someone, a fat woman in a shapeless mac, and he's shaking his head. He tips his neck back and I just know what he's doing. Already I can see those eyes rolling their way towards the sky and, as they both turn together and look at me, an unspeakable rage begins to unfurl somewhere in the back of my throat.

I pretend to scoop the missing poo up, slamming the lid as hard as I can down on the red bin. He's staring again. Who does he think he is? The fucking crap-police?

I start marching down the path. Burning up. Trembling. I want to kill him. I muster all the strength I can in my feeble arms and throw Scrappy's blue ball towards him, the desire to launch it at grey-beard almost overpowering. I gasp for air, that familiar breathless sensation warning me that I'm not capable of the bitter verbal attack I long to fell him with.

I gasp again. The base of my throat makes a horrible wheezing sound. I'm struggling to breathe, but I'm nearly behind him now. I'm going to ram Scrappy's ball right into the back of greybeard's legs. Bring him down to his knees. Bastard.

'HOW FUCKING DARE YOU!' I'm going to scream. 'You fucking, fucking, fucker, I'm dying!'

But, of course, I don't. I can't. What will come out will mean that his worst fears are confirmed – I am a nutter. And not just an ordinary one, but a dangerous, irresponsible one who leaves her own dog's faeces to fester in the grass.

I storm ahead as he turns left with the woman, the horrible honking noises of my crying mingling with the drizzle.

Since PEG and pneumonia, I know that Mildred is getting stronger and I sob all the way across the park. How far along am I on the dying line now? That's what I want to know. The grey sky presses down as I stop by a tree, leaning against it to catch my breath. Scrappy huddles against my legs as the rain descends.

When I saw my neurologist two weeks ago, I tried to catch him out on the subject of my mortality. I try and ask this question each time I go, but as ever, his evasive grin and shrug gives me his answer. He doesn't know and doesn't want to speculate, so his lips stay firmly closed. I know he's not a fortune teller, but I want him to know, to say something, anything. However, this time, whilst admiring my iPad 2 with its cute stripy cover, I thought I might be able to slip in that 'how long have I got?' question whilst he wasn't paying Mildred much attention.

But no. He wasn't going to be caught out. He smiled his sweet little smile again and said nothing.

'I'll see you in three months then, Mrs Jones.' He shook my hand.

Outside I bump into someone from our local support group. 'Hey, Eric.' It was so comforting to find a fellow sufferer, that I flung my arms around him.

We share a joke about PEGs and how he was asked what flavour nourishment drink he would like to put into his feeding tube.

'Like I could taste it!'

We laugh far too loudly.

Here, nearing home, I'm trying to do my calm breathing from the stomach, not the chest. In, out, in, out. I don't want to blubber and dribble in front of my sons; it's difficult enough for them to watch me fading.

Ordinary tasks are getting harder. I struggle to turn the key in the lock. My fingers fumble with the catch on my handbag. The poppers on my coat refuse to move. I wipe the remaining tears from my face and close the door.

'Hi,' I gurgle.

Owen is still in bed but Robbie is in the front room and as I struggle to pull my weak arms out of the jacket sleeves, he appears in the doorframe.

'Mum?'

I burst into tears.

'Mum, what's wrong?'

He puts his arm round me as I type out on my iPad about my close encounter with the horrible man. Just as I finish, Scrappy brings 'bally' out from my bag and lays it at our feet. We can't help but laugh.

Robbie suggests, as therapy, that I catch up on the episodes of *The Bill* that I've missed, and to try not to wallow.

I try. But wallowing is all I can do at the moment. If I had one foot in the stirrup after Christmas, I am now face down in the mud with my horse across the other side of a huge field. I'm not sure if I even have the strength to heave myself back in the saddle. But I suppose for my family, I do need to try.

Chapter Thirteen

Just My Imagination

Mildred

•

I don't know where Robbie conjured up 'Mildred' from when I'd asked him at Christmas to give Motor Neurone a name. But later, when I asked Owen if he remembered how we'd once named scary insects to help Robbie with his fears, he, too, came straight out with 'William Wasp'. He also reminded me, somewhat smugly, that he had never been scared of creepy crawlies and had once asked if he could have a pet tarantula. (The scream of 'No!' even managing to bring Gareth out from behind his newspaper.) But anyway... Owen gave a slight pause and then said, very confidently, 'Maud', a name in my view equally quirky and old fashioned, yet strangely more sorrowful than 'Mildred'.

In my twenties, I had a phase of reading the tragic life stories of various troubled, yet glamorous, Hollywood film stars. *Mildred Pierce* is one of my favourite films from this era and this made it inevitable that the physical appearance of Mildred was going to be a sort of 1940's movie star, a cross between Bette Davies and Joan Crawford. Someone you wouldn't dream of crossing, someone who, with one of her terrifying gazes, could crush you into submission.

Out walking Scrappy, a few days after I had finished Chapter 12, I was feeling more upbeat and wondering whether what I had written was a bit too dark and that readers might wind up wishing I had never started with this morbid little tale in the first place.

The sun had finally emerged from the clouds after days and days of rain, and I sat down on a park bench whilst Scrappy gnawed on his blue ball and contemplated the pigeons with a disappointed air. Though grey in colour, they were not 'sqiwells', and didn't play chase with him. Mulling over my writing and deciding that I might have to either rewrite or remove Chapter 12, I let my mind wander. Then I heard a voice, one distinctly different than mine, and she was speaking to me. I might have been crossing over into the dark side at that point, but I knew who it was, all right. So here it is: Chapter 13.

'Jeez girl, I thought you said this wasn't going to be a goddamn misery memoir.'

A tall, slim woman stands in the doorframe. Dark, heavily made-up eyes peer out from behind a sweep of sleek hair that falls over her right shoulder. She tilts her head towards the ceiling and inhales deeply on a cigarette. Her nails are bright red and sharply pointed.

'Who? What?...' Unexpectedly clear words echo around the plain, white walls of the room. I am sitting in a red leather chair in a room without windows. The light on the ceiling is bright and unforgiving.

'Ah gee, don't give me that old baloney, you know who I am.'

Her voice is deep, melodic and very American.

'Mildred... Mildred?' She smiles a coy, almost flirtatious smile.

'Yep, that's the one.' She moves very slightly towards me, staring so intensely that her eyes turn black.

'This last one, Chapter 12... mmmm. I think you've been reading too much Sylvia Plath again, as this is de-press-ing. Only you could make a drama out of some old guy in a park who's just trying to be a good citizen.'

'I was down. Right down. He upset me... I tried to make it funny, but well...'

'Ha, ha.' She blows on to one of her red nails, as if ready to rip something, or someone, to pieces. I wait for her to start roaring.

'I mean... don't you think you're being a little hard on me? I'm not all bad.' She touches her hair, stroking it over her ear. 'I mean... well, think about it.'

Think about it? The nerve. The sheer audacity of her. Not being able to talk or eat, not that bad? To have to rely on a plastic tube to keep me alive? That rage again, the one from the park, leaps into life.

'Hard on you? You're killing me, and not even very... softly.' She ignores my feeble attempt at a joke. 'In fact the word I would use is "cruelly". Yes, killing me cruelly, that's what you're doing to me.'

She is studying me more closely now. I watch her jaw muscles flicker and twitch, but then she moves her lips into a little smile and nods her head.

'Put it like that kiddo and I must admit it sucks, but well, I have given you some time... I mean, you could have gone straight away.' She motions as if she is cutting her throat. 'Say, a heart attack, or car crash. It's all about the way you see it.'

'Great. Slow and lingering versus short and sudden. Some choice.'

'Oh boy, you are on a downer today. What about Scrappy? You wouldn't have him for a start? And without me in your life, you might not have had anything to write about or met all those great people on the Memoir Writing course?'

'True, but...' There's no stopping Mildred now.

'And all the love you've been shown? And the chance for you to fix things with people? I've seen how it's worked out, some stuff has been healed, right?'

'I guess so, yes, but...'

'You don't wanna die.'

Looking around, I notice, for the first time, a sign in the corner displaying: The Waiting Room, please respect this place.

'No.'

I am crying now, of course. Big, heaving, messy sobs.

She steps forward and places a hand on my shoulder. It is shockingly warm.

'No one wants to die, hun, but... heck, you humans all have to go one day. The trouble is you don't believe it.' The room begins to darken. Faint shadows appear on the walls. Mildred shivers...

'It's nothing you did, you know, your name just came up in the health lottery. You got me, I'm afraid. Bad luck.' She pats my back gently, the way a mother would.

'Will it hurt?'

'What, dying? No, sweetie, not with me. It's a fading. You know... a few lights, a bit of mist... that's all. '

She steps backwards; my shoulder feels lonely without her.

'I need to go but you make sure you keep writing heh?'

'But... how long? How long have I...?'

She's moving now, melting. Sliding into the shadows.

'Mildred – wait.'

Too late.

'I'll be seeing you kid...' She sinks into the whiteness as her voice fades, and I close my eyes.

The Jones family (from left): *Gareth, Lindy, Robbie and Owen. July 2012.*

Lindy (left), *Viv and Mum.*

Wedding day – Albert Barcroft and Mary Jay.

Mary Barcroft (far left) *with Margary and sister, Elsie.*

Mum with Karey, Viv, Lindy, Frauka, the au pair, outside the tool shed at Ravensdale.

Lindy, Mum, Granny and Viv.

Lindy with baby Karey.

Left. Back row, (l to r): Mum, Uncle Eric and cousin Geoffrey. Front row, (l to r): Karey, Grandma Cathy and Aunty Julie.

Lindy, riding Gaylad.

The Lucas family, the photograph written about in chapter 7.

Lindy, the young reader.

Our house in Ravensdale Avenue.

Lindy, age fourteen.

Lindy and Viv.

(L to r): *Karey, Viv and Lindy.*

Keith McMullan and Andrew Bonito.

Graduation day with Mum.

Teaching at William Gladstone, early 1980s.

Lindy, with Robbie and Owen.

Lindy and Jill (Smith)Vonberg.

Mike (at bottom), Edmonton.

(L to r): Cousin Sheila, cousin Cathy and sister Karey.

Paul (in red sweater) Ch. 6.

Omari's graduation.

Visit to Globe Theatre with Cheshunt 6th formers.

Google (left) *and Scrappy.*

(L to r): *Robbie, Lindy and Owen.*

Lindy on holiday in Devon.

Chapter Fourteen

Keeping it in the Family

May 2012

•

I have sunk into depression and am back to crying periodically on the sofa throughout the day, sobbing and typing out despairing phrases to Molly when she comes to see me. I don't reply to any e-mails or texts, I just want to curl up and miraculously resume my former healthy life.

I try and phone the hospice to speak to my palliative care nurse, Joan, who has assured me that all the care team understand my speech and know who I am. Hmmm.

'Nor' 'undon hospish?' I slurp, wishing my mouth didn't always feel so full of slime.

There is a pause and so I try again. 'Ish at a hospish?'

'You got the wrong number!' Shouts a deep, male voice immediately. Then: 'What the bloody hell was that?' he says, presumably to someone nearby.

That?

Fucking hell, have I become a 'that'?

Heaving self-pitying sobs.

Later on, the phone rings and thinking it might be Joan, I decide to answer it.

'Hewo,'

'Hello?' The voice is suspiciously cheery, which can only mean one thing.

'Hewo?'

'Mrs Jones, my name's Sean, how are you today?'

A fucking cold caller, that's all I need.

'I ill.'

'Er, sorry, didn't quite catch that. My name is Sean, I hope I haven't caught you at a bad moment.'

'I 'ying,' I gurgle into the receiver.

'Sorry, Mrs Jones, the line's a little unclear.'

'I 'ying.' [I'm dying.]
'You don't sound well, are you all right?'
'No!' my inner bitch shouts before I can stop her.
'Well, perhaps you should sit down then, take it easy, Mrs
Jones, goodbye.' He slams the phone down and I can almost
hear his sigh of relief.

Piss off and leave me alone, I scream in my head as I imagine
him telling the other people at the call centre about this crazy
woman he spoke to today.

I throw the phone down and weep beside Scrappy, who
licks my eyelids tenderly.

The week passes in a miserable, grey, rainy way. I even put
the heating on one evening. My sister, Karey, and cousins,
Sheila and Cathy, are due to visit me from 'up north' on the
Saturday and I need to pull myself together.

Unusual for this miserable wet summer, the sun makes a brief
appearance when they arrive, laden with bulky bags full of childhood diaries and a massive bunch of lilies. The mood barometer,
which has been on minus 10 for the past week, slowly starts to
rise.

My sister bounces in first and gives me a massive hug. We
haven't seen each other since February and since then I've lost
another stone.

'Wow, slim Lindy,' she says with just a touch of sisterly envy
in her voice. 'Hello, Scrappy, do you remember Auntie Karey?'
Scrappy is sniffing her bulging bag, hopeful that it might con-
tain something edible, so he wags his tail politely on hearing
his name.

Soon we have settled in the front room fussing over Scrappy.
'Come on girls, get the diaries out.'

Karey and Sheila pull several thick diaries from their bags.
'I wish I'd kept one,' Cathy says, eyeing up my three carefully
written page-a-day diaries: 1969, 1970 1971.

Sheila and I find the week we stayed in Nelson with Grandma
and Grandpa in 1969.

'Hey, Lindy,' Sheila says, scrolling through her thick green
diary, 'do you remember going to The Imperial in Nelson?'

I shake my head but pick up my pink 1969 diary and open

the pages as brown bits of sellotape and old bus tickets flutter to the ground.

'Karey, can you read this?' I type, already beginning to giggle at the strange drawing I had done of Sheila and stuck in the diary.

She clears her throat and perches on the edge of the sofa as if she's about to read a story to a bunch of unruly school kids.

Sunday 25th May
No one was dancing to any Tamla Motown except Sheila and I raving it up. There were loads of vile rockers there doing Rock n Roll. All the girls were vile sluts.

We all snort with laughter as Karey tries to read more.

Wednesday 28th May
We got wet in the rain going to 'The Imperial'. One nasty greaser bent down to kiss me, I screamed and pushed him away. Then a big greasy troublemaker with hipster jeans, bent and whispered something to me.
We saw Ivan, but the other creepy wasn't there. One bloke trod on Sheila's toe, I told him to buzz off. A tall lanky queer kept asking her to dance.

'Oh, God, this is too funny to read out,' she eventually manages to say, wiping her eyes whilst I have to mop up the drool from my rasping messy wheeze which passes for laughter these days. Sheila and Cathy are clutching each other on the sofa, Sheila's loud uncontrollable cackle drowning the rest of us out.

'Who was Ivan?' Karey asks red-faced and breathing heavily when she finally manages to speak.

No idea, I shrug, mopping at my chin.

'According to my diary I'd arranged to meet some boys on the Monday but we didn't want to go, I mean, why did we then?' Sheila lifts her head from the pages of neat backward slanting scrawl.

'I've found the bit here,' says Karey, lifting my tatty diary up once more.

... feeling sick at heart and very depressed we walked slowly there. They came – I felt like crying. We got on a bus to Rough-lee. It was shut so we went back to Nelson. We were so relieved.

'Oh, God Lindy what did you do? Just go on a bus?'
'No memory of it,' I type.
'All these vile sluts you keep writing about! You snob,' Karey says as she scans the pages.
'Oh listen to this,' says Sheila.

Lindy and I talked about our terrible depressions and mood swings and wondered if it can be passed down in the family as Grandma and both our mums have had depression. Perhaps it's in our blood.

This triggered off a discussion about our grandma, and what had happened to turn her into such an eccentric, germ-obsessed woman.
'I remember all her names,' announces Cathy.
'Oh yes, me too,' says Karey, and they both chant:
'Annie, Mariya, Matilda, Sophia, Victoria, Marjorie, Nancy, Doris, Clara Mary, Evelyn Jay.' It has a poetic little rhythm to it, particularly the – Mariya/Sophia – pronounced like the word 'sapphire'.
Grandma had told us all that this was because her parents couldn't decide what to call her, and all four of us can still, more or less, recite the names forty years later.
The afternoon passes too quickly and then it's time for them to leave.
I feel sad waving them goodbye; the house quiet after all the noisy laughter. With everyone out I think I might take advantage of a peaceful house and do some writing. I re-read the last chapter, pleased with my characterisation of Mildred, but am not in the mood to continue with her, so I start looking through my old diaries.
I type out a list of all the years I've covered, as there are gaps where I have destroyed them, not wishing my sons to read about my little adventures when young and irresponsible. But

what am I going to do with them? And will anyone give a flying fuck after I've snuffed it to read entries such as: *Weight - 9 stone 3 - alc - two glasses of wine - spent all day marking coursework...* This is obviously something I need to think about.

Letter

•

I might well be a somewhat unreliable narrator, so I asked my family and a few friends to share their impressions of the Lindy they know. Here is the first of their contributions, though it has to be said, as you will see, that everyone is far too complimentary. Still I guess it's as near as I'll get to being at my own funeral – shame I won't be able to enjoy the booze-up. This letter is from my sister, Karey Lucas Hughes.

I don't have many memories of Lindy as a child because of the six-year gap between our ages. This means that by the time my childhood memories start (around age six) Lindy was already at secondary school and becoming a rather moody teenager.

As children, I vaguely remember all three of us putting on puppet shows in the lounge, behind some big curtains. We had several beautiful wooden stringed puppets. I think one was an ugly witch, with a sparkly dress. I also remember hiding behind the sofa with my siblings, while watching 'Doctor Who' and running around 'the Jelly Chair.'

As a teenager, I remember Lindy looking like Mary Hopkin with long, blonde hair parted in the middle and hippy style clothes. In the days before straighteners, she used to iron her hair to make it straighter! Also, she taught me how to burn off split ends by twisting hair and then running a lighted taper down the length of it!

Lindy had a big 'Afghan' sheepskin coat with wool trimmings that smelt of old goat – especially after it rained. She influenced me and my brother a lot in both her clothes and music taste. We looked up to her and basically copied her. I remember her sewing velvet triangles into straight jeans to make them flared and then sewing lampshade tassels on the bottom to make a fringe. My brother and I both did the same. Lindy also pioneered the wearing of desert boots and 'Loon' trousers in different colours. I found a letter she wrote from college recently, in which she asked me to go to Hampstead to get her some red clogs. She even sent me the money (a mere £8!!). I copied her clog wearing too!

Lindy introduced my brother and me to The Grateful Dead by playing 'Workingman's Dead' over and over one summer. As a result, my brother and I went to see them at Alexandra Palace in 1974 – when I was thirteen!! (Lindy didn't go with us – she was probably away at uni.) Lindy also went to Southgate Technical College to do her 'A'-Levels and had a gap year before they were even invented so my brother and I both did that too!

I was perhaps most influenced by Lindy in her diary writing and reading. She used to write lots and stick in tickets, pictures and memorabilia and I did the same. We even used to secretly read each other's diaries – in which we both admitted to reading each other's diaries!

I also read the Brontë sisters' novels because Lindy had read them; she is a 'Wuthering Heights' fan while I prefer 'Jane Eyre'. I think she thought of herself as the passionate, tormented Emily, while I felt myself to be the quieter, plainer, more pragmatic Charlotte. At college, she wrote a dissertation on Sylvia Plath which I read. As a result, I became very interested in Plath, her life and poetry.

When I was still at school, aged about fifteen, Lindy wrote letters to me from Brighton about her student life, giving very thoughtful, 'sisterly' observations about parties and relationships and growing up – whilst being sure to point out how boring my life was! Age sixteen, after O-Levels, I visited her there once in her flat in Pool Valley and had such a good time I chose to go to Brighton when I decided to do teacher training.

It is a terrible blow to all of us in the family, that Lindy has got MND, and so relatively young. I miss hearing her voice and listening to her funny stories – she has always been able to make us all laugh! I don't think she has ever realised what influence she had on her siblings. I have certainly always looked up to her and followed her lead. In the most difficult of circumstances, she is still blazing her own, unique, passionate trail.

Chapter Fifteen

Grandma

•

In the memory box I have for mum, there is a four-sided typed piece of writing, which formed part of a job application; this is an extract from it.

My understanding that mental suffering could seriously affect a person's ability to enjoy life began when I was in my early teens. My mother, who had always been fussy about hygiene, became increasingly obsessed with it. She started boiling combs, brushes, and even an alarm clock once, indeed any article that she deemed to have been contaminated with germs but whilst she sterilised, the house became full of dust and fluff.

My mother's 1970's statement to support her application to work as a social worker in Haringey. At the time, we three children were in Secondary school and mum felt that her ten years at home had been quite enough.

As a child, whenever my grandma (Mary) came down from 'up north' to stay during the school holidays, my brother, sister and I would constantly have our slovenly hygiene habits criticised. The air was punctuated with her cries of 'wash your paws now', before and after eating, even if it was only a humble apple. The problem was that this hand washing could go on for a long time, far too long in fact, when there were other things we wanted to do, such as tease and fight with each other.

Excessive and repetitive soaping, rinsing, soaping, rinsing, resulted in her poor hands being red and cracked. The gold wedding ring cut so tightly into her swollen finger that I worried endlessly about the pain it must cause her. But grandma merely laughed, reassuring me it didn't hurt one bit.

Grandma was not only a bit bonkers but also a giggler and would begin each laugh with 'Eh' – said in a deep Lancashire accent – before her whole body began to shake. She would spend hours playing with us: cards, Ludo, or Snakes and Ladders, whilst she told us about her 'voices'.

She always called my brother, Viv, Jack Brabham – a racing driver at the time – but we had absolutely no idea why. It seemed crazy, but utterly fascinating and hilarious, that every night she saw a huge, white Michelin X Man who would come and sit at the end of her bed for a good chat.

She would take us to all the Disney films about animals, such as *Old Yeller* and *The Incredible Journey*, munching her way through a big bag of sweets. Afterwards, walking home I'd notice sweat trickling down her face, but taking off her raincoat was out of the question. Someone might look at her fat stomach.

Talking to grandma was a sidesplitting experience because of her deafness due to working in the cotton mills. Like the Saucepan Man in *The Magic Faraway Tree* who constantly misheard words, our conversations might run along such lines as:

– Grandma, would you like some cheese?
– What? You've got fleas?
– No, CHEESE!
– You want to sneeze?

(Ironically, I now frequently have these kinds of conversations with my family.)

One incident that still makes me and cousin Sheila laugh was when we were staying for a holiday with grandma and grandpa in Nelson. We were teenagers and, wanting to make sure we didn't miss the coach, Sheila called out from the bedroom:

'Grandma, have you set the alarm clock?'

At which point we heard her say:

'Albert, I think the girls have got something stuffed up their noses, go and see what's wrong'

Eventually, when granddad appeared we simply couldn't reply, we were laughing so much.

But to the adults, grandma was a serious cause for concern. As her grandchildren, we had no idea of the depression she suffered from or that hearing voices was very serious. And at some point, the medical world decided that a 'procedure' was needed. A part of her brain was deemed to be causing these malfunctions and if a bit of it was removed, she would, apparently, become a much happier and saner woman. (Not much, it turned out.)

I can still remember going to collect her from the hospital after she'd had the lobotomy, not really understanding why or what it was. 'Obsessive thoughts, delusions, depression and anxiety', were some of the words used by psycho dad when, as an older teenager, I asked him about her. But it was her sad little baldhead that upset me most – the half-shaven skull revealing a pink scar with a small row of stitches, neatly positioned at the base of her hairline. Poor grandma.

'Of course, she'd never been happy with Albert,' mum told me one evening as we sipped our gins and orange. I was now twenty-one and grandma was in a nursing home. Becoming a 'grown-up' meant joining my parents, if I was home from Teacher Training College, for a 'cocktail' at six. Tonight though, it was just me and mum.

'Grandma and grandpa quarrelled the whole time. Mother would put the supper on, leave it to boil dry and then laugh when Albert complained.' Mum took another sip, her pale skin flushed with alcohol. 'And she used to boil all the coins in his pockets, his front pockets,' she intonated, leaning forward. 'You know, that they were close to his... *penis*.' Oh, God, my granddad had a penis, please no, I didn't want to know.

'I don't think they ever enjoyed sex.'

'Really?' I was both repulsed and fascinated by the thought of Albert, the shrivelled grumpy old man who barely spoke, having sexual feelings. I took another nervous sip. I was not at all comfortable with this subject and hoped like fuck that mum wasn't about to reveal any details of her sex life to me.

'She was very beautiful when she was young, your Grandma.' I nodded, and she added, 'But Albert was a bit of a womaniser. I hated their quarrelling and made up my mind at sixteen that I didn't want to marry anyone with a bad temper.'

These revelations were astonishing. I took another, bigger sip; the gin was starting to have an effect. What ambitions did my twenty-one-year-old self have? I hadn't even given a thought to what kind of man I would marry. I just naturally assumed I too would live in a large, four-bedroomed house, and have holidays abroad and plenty of money, but that was about it. I was just waiting to find 'the one' and then everything would fall perfectly into place.

Albert failed to mend poor Mary's broken heart and he became more angry and frustrated by the blackened pans and by her fixation on germs.

'"Eee, Albert, I've burnt your tea again," Mary would announce before bursting into laughter and enraging her eldest daughter Sheila. Personally, I found it highly amusing but daren't ever laugh.' Mum took the whole issue of her mother's negligence of Albert's nutritional needs extremely seriously.

Cut to another early evening chat with mum on the subject of grandma's life which I found utterly compelling.

'She had a man friend, too.' This expression had me snorting out my gin and orange.

'What? She was having an affair?' The skeletons were really coming out to play now.

'No, not really, I remember this man coming to the house, he'd bring sandwiches for her, she was hopeless at looking after herself... but Albert didn't like this.'

As mum got up to draw the curtains, I began to think how romantic and sweet it was, that this man who had a crush on Mary would lovingly slice bread and butter it for her, to make sure she ate at lunchtime. Trying to imagine any of my past boyfriends at college in this caring role was impossible. Rolling you a fag or wrenching open a can of lager maybe, but worrying about whether you were eating enough food, not a chance.

Settling herself back into the sofa mum continued, 'I mean she loved us very much. She took us out for picnics, read to us... but... she was like a child in some ways and what she always wanted was a boy... but Albert...' her voice trailed into a full stop.

'Albert... what, Mum?'

'Oh, I shouldn't tell you.'

'Mum, please, I'm an adult now, not a child.'

'Well, I was about sixteen and Grandma got pregnant again. Margaret was fourteen and Julie, six.'

'And?' I sat forward, tense and slightly pissed.

'Albert... Albert made her get rid of it.'

'Oh, my God, but weren't they illegal?'

'Yes, but women... you know... did them... And it was a boy, the baby, Grandma was in a terrible state.'

'Bloody hell. Oh, God, she must have...' I couldn't speak it. The baby must have been a few months old. Jesus.

'Poor Mother, she never really recovered. After that the house just got dirtier and dirtier.'

It was all past my understanding that a woman could be put into such an awful situation. No wonder she retreated into a world of voices. But was this true? I found it all crazy. Too terrible to even imagine.

And then I understand.

Mary is at the stove, her pretty face reddened with heat. She's boiling the coins, throwing them mercilessly into a pan on the stove. One by one, out of the trouser pockets they fly as she cries and cries for her lost son.

Chapter Sixteen

A Guided Tour of My Childhood Home

•

Dear Reader,

In my old life, whenever anyone asked me to spell my name Lindy after I'd said the letter 'Y', I would have this terrible, overwhelming urge to say 'Is a custard pie'. This is what my brother, Viv, used to tease me with when we were children. It has stuck in my head all these years, along with the memory of carving my name with a penknife into the back of a wooden chair where I'd sit, glowering with brooding 'older sister' eyes' at my annoying brother, and even more annoying baby sister, Karey, who is five years younger than me.

71 Ravensdale Avenue, London N12 9HR
Phone number: Hillside 6586
Bought for £4,500 in 1959.

A spacious, four-bedroomed semi-detached house on a corner with a large back garden and garage.

The Tool Shed

•

I think it had originally been an old air-raid shelter but now it is stuffed with all sorts of weird things. In here, my pet rat, Tara, scurries desperately up and down her cage, gnawing at the cardboard lid in a bid for freedom. Various mice bearing names like 'Flicka' and 'Kinky' have also lived here as well as a gerbil, loads of my dad's tools, various old cupboards, and bags of sawdust, straw and rabbit food. It's quite a creepy place, full of dark unlit cobwebbed corners. A single, bare bulb hangs ominously from the ceiling. I definitely do not like coming in here when it's dark, there are far too many odd shapes and unknown places.

The Outside Toilet
•

A damp, spidery place between the kitchen and the tool shed. We send dad there every morning because no one else likes using it. This is mainly because of the large, hairy spiders that like to crawl out from behind the collection of old boots just as you have forced yourself to sit on the cold, enamel seat.

In my teenage years it became infamous for the 'Wellington boot full of wee' that mum nearly put her foot into the Sunday morning after a particularly drunken gathering the night before. This toilet is also the place where I was once so violently sick after a party that the next-door neighbours shouted over from their garden to make sure I was all right.

The Kitchen
•

Mum keeps her love letters from dad in a faded box in the pantry. She takes them out to read sometimes, so I'm always careful as a nosy teenager to put them back carefully after I've sneaked a look. But the trouble is that dad's handwriting is so awful, I can't make out much at all other than 'Darling Sheila', which sounds amazingly romantic.

We often eat round the table in the kitchen, Perdy has her bed in the corner and mum wrestles with pots and pans in her 'laboratory', as she calls it. She is a good cook, but messy. Recipe books are streaked with multi-coloured smears of gravy or sauce, while the cupboards and drawers are stuffed with odd things.

Me, Viv and Karey squabble round this table until mum gets angry and shouts. She can be quite scary when she's in a mood or, worse, has 'the Face' on, so then we just mouth silent curses at each other, or pull faces.

Perdy is totally terrified of mum so never, ever, tries to beg for food when she's around. When dad comes in from work through the back door of the kitchen after parking his car in the garage, mum is always happy and usually has a drink waiting for him. They call each 'Twee' and 'Too-Too'. Mum is 'Twee', but she also calls dad, 'Tiffy', short for 'Christopher'.

They really get on my nerves when they are all lovey-dovey. It was the kitchen where mum broke her toe slipping on a pool of dog sick left by Perdy after she scoffed down a huge box of chocolates someone had left out.

The kitchen is also a sad place. My guinea pigs were found dead in it one morning and the oven is where dad put my mouse, Flicka, to sleep because she had a huge tumour. We placed her in a shoebox full of cotton wool, turned the gas on and then buried her in the garden.

The Garden

•

Here can often be found German granny, whose disapproving looks and serious tutting about the state of the scruffy flower-beds cause her to visit us for regular weeding and pruning. She arrives with her garden gloves and hat, bemoaning my dad's feeble horticultural skills.

My favourite part of the garden though, is the enormous tree at the bottom next to the garage. When I was young, the hilly base of it, combined with some bushes, formed a ready-made den where Katy Gunn, my best friend, and I would spend hours garbed in strange exotic clothes from the dressing-up box. As a moody teenager you'd often find me lying on my back on the lawn with the sun on my face listening to the sound of its whispering leaves that sang of the pleasures and freedoms awaiting me as a grown-up.

Dad has built an outside run for the rabbits so that they can scamper around on the grass away from the cages, which I think are much too small. It is a three-sided triangular shape that can easily be lifted up. One night, scuttling across the garden in the dark, he falls headlong over it, arriving in the kitchen covered in bits of old grass. We all fall about laughing as poor dad brushes the leaves and mud off his suit. For once, dad almost seems cross, which is very unusual for him.

It is my job to feed and clean out the rabbits – Moonlight, huge and white, with pink eyes, Crackers, an even bigger one with an unpredictable wildness about her, and Lara, who is smaller and meant to be sister Karey's responsibility. Fat chance. Every few weeks, dad and I go to a builder's yard to collect bags of sawdust, I clean the rabbits out once a week because I am the caring and conscientious one and the only person who can lift crazy Crackers out of her cage and hold her whilst dad trims her nails with pliers. I am proud of my way with animals and imagine that one day I will live in the countryside and have a horse and at least three dogs.

During the summer mum can often be found lying sunbathing in the garden, whereas I prefer to stay in the house reading. I don't like hot sun or insects – particularly wasps. My friends and I collect rose petals, put them into bottles and mix them up with some sort of liquid which creates a 'perfume'.

I make houses out of stones for fairies and I am terribly excited when I find a note and a drawing of 'The Fairy Queen' thanking me. Sometimes, I even find money left inside the house. Of course, I know it's mummy, because only she can draw fairies. She is artistic, not like dad, he can only manage stick-men, but he does brilliant tricks with coins and makes up really good stories about a mischievous character called 'Tricksy Gnome'.

Between the kitchen and the tool shed is a covered area where we keep our bikes. This is where Katy falls when she comes to visit. She is being treated for leukaemia and is very weak. She wears a bobble hat to hide her baldhead and she is different. Now bloated and quiet, we don't giggle anymore about 'Monsieur Le Pussycat', whoever he was. When she falls over, her leg quickly succumbs to an enormous, inky bruise. Mum rushes out with cotton wool and witch hazel, because she is a nurse and knows what to do when people get hurt. I am scared of Katy now.

My Brother Viv's bedroom
·

I am jealous of my sweet, calm brother, so I tell him that there are gorillas hiding in his cupboards waiting to come out and get him when it's dark. He has an imaginary friend called 'Mr Wolf', who I also tease him about. When I make him cry, mum smacks me on the legs for being mean.

In the cupboard is the dressing up box. My best piece of clothing is a black velvet jacket with embroidered gold-thread on it. Our favourite game is to parade around the front garden in various eccentric dresses, hats and shawls, until a car comes by and then we run into the back garden to hide.

In the aquarium by the window, is an African Toad. Dad brought him home when he was tiny and black. But one day we find him floating dead on his back with what looked like a bee-sting in his stomach.

I sleep in this room on bunk beds with my brother so that our au pairs can have their own room. But at eight years of age, I move into my own bedroom and my sister has to share with my brother. Good. Later on she has her own bedroom which I sneak into to read her diary. Once, I find, in my sister's neatly written handwriting, a confession of guilt: 'Have just been into Lindy's room to read her diary.' The cheek, I think, as I place her heavy, brown diary back by her bed.

The Cloakroom

Next to the kitchen it is the most untidy place you can imagine. The whole floor is awash with shoes, the walls thick with coats. It's a brilliant place for Hide-and-seek, as you can wrap yourself up inside the coats. But best of all there is a small window at the end, which joins onto the dining room, so you can spy on the grown-ups, or dad when he has private patients – the loonies we call them – in there occasionally.

The Dining Room

Dad likes to play his piano in this room. He has painted it white and has piles and piles of sheet music on the top. He also comes in here to smoke, using a blue ashtray, a fascinating object with air bubbles trapped inside the glass.

I sometimes do my homework in this room and can often be heard crying and screaming over my maths. Dad is so patient; he never ever gets cross. Whilst I throw textbooks across the room and sob, he continues to speak in his calm psychoanalyst's voice no matter how infuriating and melodramatic I am.

There is a large radiogram which dad plays classical music records on. Mum likes to put the Labour Party song on really loudly. 'Da da da da, da da da da, we'll sing the 'Red Flag' once a year.' She joins in, dancing round dad, her voice sweet and melodic.

The Sitting Room
•

French windows open out onto the garden. We have green velvet curtains and a beautiful emerald-and-blue Casa Pupa rug on the floor.

This is where we play games with grandma and watch television as a family. Dad always teases me about the trail of apple cores and orange peel I leave behind me, whilst mum, sitting on a low stool, irons away at the back of the room.

As a child, in this room I am glued to programmes like *Champion the Wonder Horse*, *Lassie*, *Mr Ed* (the talking horse) and *Flipper*, later graduating to *I love Lucy* and the *Dick Van Dyke Show*. Here, I spend hours playing board games with my friend Jeanette Beavan.

My Room
•

The wallpaper is covered with people in red jackets and black riding hats, leaping over fences, because I am crazy about horses. My bookshelves are stuffed with my horse books my favourites being *The Wild Heart*, *National Velvet*, *Black Beauty*, *The Silver Brumby* and *My Friend Flicka*. My 100% favourite though is *The Wild Heart* featuring La Bruja, the fearless, wild horse whose mother dies, leaving her to fend for herself. She lives alone on the South American pampas, forever fighting against the gauchos who try to capture and tame her.

I re-read this book endlessly, weeping my way through it, as La Bruja limps off to freedom at the end. Secretly, I wish I were a wild horse not a timid, plump schoolgirl.

In my desk I have loads of notebooks about horses, dreams, stories, some 'log book entries' (before I became a serious diary writer), and various poems about horses, and details about my pets.

I have a red velvet bag where I keep my small, plastic Dalmatians, because my second favourite animals are dogs. I like to have Perdy sleep on my bed which mum objects to because she thinks it is unhygienic – until a séance which I have with my cousins Sheila, Stephanie and Jacqueline in Lancashire gives me such sleepless nights that she relents.

Sometimes I also have pet mice in my room.

Here is an extract from a notebook about them. Please note that the mice are given horsey classifications. Skewbald is brown-and-white, and palomino is a pale golden colour.

My mice – Dead

Kinky – little skewbald with a kinky tail
Brandy – palomino, very friendly
Flicka – palomino, had baby
Snip – brown mouse, small with white snip, very sweet
Whiskey – brother, brown all over, very sweet
Twitch – daughter of Flicka and Brandy, terribly friendly and affectionate
Coco and Coffee – twins by Kirsty, black mouse and Snip, dark brown, gorgeous.

My mice - Alive

Whitey – little white one, very timid
Kirsty – black, quite friendly

In my notebooks, I draw horses. I list names I would call my own horse. At twelve, my school friends are mad about boys but I am still mad about horses. In lessons, I daydream about owning 'Nameless', the horse I ride at the stables each week. I think my friends are soulless idiots. I much prefer animals to humans.

A Guided Tour of My Childhood Home

My Parents' Bedroom

•

It is huge. It has wonderful slippery wooden floors where we perform ice skating shows for mum and dad. We're all dressed up and sliding in our socks over the smooth floorboards.

Mum has a black Singer sewing machine where she makes us clothes; dad has the entire works of Sigmund Freud on his bookshelf, as well as various other psycho titles such as *The Wish to Fall Ill*, which fascinates me though I don't understand a word of it. I mean, why would anyone want to be ill?

The Garage

•

It is at the end of the garden near the tree. We have two cars – a small, brown automatic Daf that dad drives into London where he works at University College as Head of Student Health, and a blue Dormobile that mum drives and which we use for holidays. Mum ferries us and our friends around in it, wrenching at the gear stick and swearing, something that deeply shocks Christine, a girl from school I brought home to tea. After mum yells 'Jesus Christ in Fucking Hell' as we take a corner sharply on the way home, the poor terrified girl, already fearful of psycho dad's supposed ability to read minds, never comes back.

No one wears a safety belt, but mum drives us round the quiet streets of 1960's Finchley for years in our Dormobile without mishap. Mum and dad drive us across France for camping holidays where the three of us fight and squabble in the back, until mum turns round to try and slap our legs.

Dad uses the Daf to take me to Mrs Jones' riding stables in Totteridge. I love being led around on Princess who is very lively, or 'gay', as we would say in those days. (I have, according to my diaries, ridden a lot of gay horses in my time.) Dad sits in the car and reads the newspaper while he waits. I love riding but am also quite scared of horses with their rolling eyes and tendency to gallop off at the sight of a plastic bag.

The Dormobile is also the place where mum tells me that my best friend, Katy Gunn, is dead. She was seven, like me.

I don't really understand death and ask if I can have her doll. I don't go to the funeral.

Sometimes, as an adult, I drive past my old house and a few years ago took dad to look at it. We felt sad, though. The flowers from the front garden have all gone, the paintwork is cracked and shabby. Despite sometimes imagining I might one day knock on the door and ask if I can look round, I know I never will.

Letter

•

From my brother, Viv Lucas.

I've always looked up to My Big Sister (MBS). As a child, a three-and-a-half-year age gap seemed huge. Wow, how grown up and mature she seemed. I was closer in age to My Little Sister (MLS). The age gap created a little distance and mystery and MBS became the person I looked up to. So much was I in awe of her that when she told me to eat a nice tomato sandwich, I dutifully did, although it was really a piece of soap (so I am told). Our psychoanalyst father would have informed us that the power of suggestion can be very strong.

When I think back to my time at primary school I don't really remember MBS being there very much. I was in the infants, she in the juniors. When I entered the juniors, she left to go to Big School. At home I remember playing together with plastic animals, changing their colours with Magic Marker pens, and putting on little plays for Mum when she was ill. MBS started her career as a drama queen then. Mum loved the sun and France and as a family we went to St Tropez on a camping holiday in 1967, the 'Summer of Love' - what a magnificent thing to do - with 'Whiter Shade of Pale' being played endlessly on the jukebox. We all had 'rubber rings' with an animal head. One of us had a swan. Whether it was me or MBS I can't be sure. Dad also bought us an orange inflatable canoe that we messed about in it, cooling off in the sea as MBS was always 'sweating, boiling and gasping'. MBS was becoming a swan whilst MLS and I remained cygnets.

Holiday memories are scant because MBS stopped coming with us from quite an early age. She had a surrogate family down in the New Forest where she would go for riding holidays. She was into horse riding. I remember going with Dad to fetch her from the stables, the smell of manure in our nostrils. For a while, following MBS, we became Horse Rangers, then, briefly, in the Woodcraft folk, a socialist alternative to the Guides and Scouts.

In our teenage years, MBS influenced me more and I was allowed to join in her parties when Mum and Dad were away; what should we do about Dad's Wellies that someone had urinated in? How grown up and sophisticated I felt, pretentiously smoking St Moritz cigarettes trying not to cough, and listening to great music – David Bowie's 'Hunky Dory', Eric Clapton's '461 Ocean Blvd', CSNY's 'Déjà Vu' and so much more. MBS introduced me to so much great music that is with me to this day. One Christmas in the early 70s she was given Neil Young's 'After the Gold Rush'. I was bowled over by this album. We once clubbed together to buy an LP as they were expensive (about two quid). I suggested The Who, 'Live at Leeds'. I pronounced 'live' as in to 'live in a house'. Lindy corrected me, sniggering a little. Perhaps The Teacher was emerging then.

For my 14th birthday MBS gave me 'The Yes Album'. Yes become my teenage music passion, overshadowing Neil Young for a while. MBS began learning the guitar. I naturally had to copy her. To this day I have a tendency to twang a guitar and let my voice quiver in a bid to emulate Neil. If anyone doesn't like this, well, they can always blame MBS.

Lindy left home to train as an English teacher in Brighton. In the summer of 1976 I visited her there. We

116

lay on the pebbly beach and I acquired badly sunburnt legs. I couldn't bear to wear trousers or walk for days. Of course I never got to see her working as a schoolteacher. It is not until recently that I have seen all the cards and letters her pupils sent her at the end of term demonstrating the affection and respect that she was held in, although lovingly acknowledged to be perhaps just a little eccentric. I had no desire to emulate her by becoming a teacher and I respect her for being able to stand up in front of a class of unruly adolescents trying to help them learn the lessons of literature.

Latterly, Lindy has taught me so much. She has taught me lessons in how to live as a person with MND. When she was first diagnosed I worried about how she would 'cope'. In time, she allayed these fears, and the love and respect of those early years grew. I shared with her some of my creative writing. She made me read passages out loud, something she could not do. We laughed at some of my clangers. 'Show, don't tell', she would say, and 'Remember, verbs are the muscles of sentences.' Well, MBS has shown me more than she could say and through the process of her own muscles weakening, a hidden inner strength emerged. And hopefully this piece is better written than it would have had I not had lessons from MBS.

Viv is much too modest about the guitar playing. I gave up as the strings hurt my fingers but Viv kept playing and now performs regularly as 'Neil Young'. He is brilliant.

Chapter Seventeen

Every Breath I Take

May 2012

•

When I was a girl, I was fascinated by a television programme called *Emergency Ward Ten*, a sort of forerunner to medical dramas like *Casualty* and *ER*. No matter what 'procedures' were used and despite the efforts by the doctors and nurses, a lot of the patients, all too frequently it seemed to me, ended up in this massive metal toilet-roll called 'The Iron Lung'.

The paralysed person would then have to spend endless days lying inside it as their lungs were induced to move so that they could breathe. All you could see was their head poking out at the end of it, but there was a small mirror fixed onto the side so the poor person could see the room, rather than having to stare continuously at the entrance to their living tomb.

I began to think about this peculiarly vile medical device on the morning of April 30th 2012, the day of my lung-function test, which I already knew I was not going to pass with flying colours. My achievement was definitely going to be more of the slow, grey variety.

Even before my dramatic aspirating episode and subsequent trolley choking turn, I had noticed changes to my breathing. Small things at first. Bending down, then straightening up, caused a weird breathless sensation. Then I had a full-blown 'help me, God, I'm dying' incident, whilst out in the park with Scrappy.

Before I'd left for our little constitutional, I'd hurriedly shoved some medication down and now, as I tramped my way through the damp February leaves, I started to sense that the pill had not gone down properly, that it was in fact wedged halfway down my throat.

I attempted to cough it up, spluttering and spitting for ages beneath the trees, willing it to pop back up. Meanwhile, oblivious to this medical drama, Scrappy was leaping around my legs for his red ball that I had flung out between gasps. But then a terrible thing came into my head. Suppose this pill did fly up back into my throat? With only my weak tongue for support, it might zoom backwards into my airway causing me to asphyxiate. My last minutes on earth would then be spent face down under the trees, sucking in dead leaves, covered in dog crap, whilst Scrappy danced around me, nudging his cheerful, wet nose into my thrashing head.

Panic was now complete and as the wretched plastic-coated pill began melting, foul-tasting liquid started to burn into the back of my throat. Bordering on hysteria, I began stumbling and gasping my way noisily across the wet grass, saliva streaming out of my mouth and over my chin. Need to reach car. Home. Home...

Leaning desperately across the bonnet, wheezing and gurgling like some poor goldfish flipped out of its water, my mouth opened and closed without any precious air going down.

'Oh, God, don't let me die, not here alone in a park, please not yet.'

And then, through the frenzy, I heard, 'Breathe from your stomach, breathe from your stomach.'

It was Fiona Osteopath's cheerful voice.

I took a slower, more successful breath. And again. Perhaps I wasn't, after all, going to die slumped over my blue Beetle at the entrance to Grovelands Park.

But it was a sign, I knew it. It was no good trying to make myself believe it was a simple panic attack. Mildred's fingers were on the move again. Sliding down through my jaw, down through my stiffening neck, down into my precious chest muscles.

For the test on this April morning, I knew what to do. I'd had lots of lung function tests in 2011, when I had been a guinea pig in a drug trial for MND. But this time, putting the rubber mouthpiece in was much harder and my annoying, floppy bottom-lip would not make an airtight seal. The woman was kind, admiring my summery top and telling me to relax, but it was like going in to do an exam that you know you are going to fail. Soon, tears were bubbling pathetically in the back of my eyes.

Breathing in very quickly and then expelling as much air as you can is designed to test your lung capacity and also, I guess, the muscle strength. The second part of this, the sniff test, was hopeless. One nostril blocked by a plastic wedge, I had to breathe in as sharply as I could, or in my case, couldn't.

'Try again, Rosalind.' I tried for the second time. 'Breathe in, hard, quickly now!' Again, my mousy little sniff was disappointing.

Outside, we were told to wait in another clinic to discuss the findings with Professor P – who I imagined would be a wise old man with curly hair and pebble glasses. Gareth nervously flicked through magazines, whilst I studied the other people imagining what might be wrong with them.

'Oh, do come in now and zit down.' A foreign-accented, grey-haired woman shakes our hands vigorously and gestures towards the chairs.

'Now, Mrs Jones, Mr Jones. Ahh, I'm afraid to tell you zat ze breathing muscle strength has deteriorated since December, but you are a perfect candidate for ze Breathing Ventilator. You see how the neck is stiff, she says to a smiley-faced blonde woman next to her wearing a physiotherapy badge.

I start crying.

'Oh, what a lovely handbag,' Professor P says, stroking its red leather as I fumble with my iPad.

'I'm worried I'm going to die soon,' I type, then turn the screen towards them.

No response.

'You see how centralized ze weakness is,' she says to Ms Physio, 'but the ventilator will be wonderful. We may even improve your speech.' She's beaming at me now.

She's so warm and enthusiastic that against my will I smile back.

'Now, you vill see us next week for a fitting, yes?'

'It will really help you,' Ms Physio says enthusiastically. They are both so sweet that for a split second I want to fall into their arms and be rescued, comforted, made better.

At home I go onto my computer and torture myself with images of people wearing these hideous Hannibal Lector masks, sobbing until I can hardly breathe, an irony not lost on me.

'I'm not fucking having one,' I type onto my iPad. 'Look!'
Gareth and Robbie peer uncomfortably at the pictures I
flash at them.

'I hate having a PEG and I'm not having... THAT!' I point,
throwing myself onto the arm of the sofa.

I remember a line from a Plath poem about things being
'over'. (Trust me to think of tragic Sylvia at this moment.)

Yes. That's fucking it. Over. I can't go on. I'm going to stop
feeding... refuse the mask... let myself fade away. A slow,
wasting suicide.

'I'm giving up, I don't want to live anymore,' I tap, whilst
Gareth and Robbie stare glumly at me, their faces tight and
helpless.

'Well, if that's what you want...' Gareth might as well be
agreeing that my bum looks big. I am furious now, furious that
he's going to allow me to die without putting up a fight.

I push roughly past them both, loudly stomping to the bedroom with noisy, gurgling screams of rage. Suffering has not
made me noble – it has released my inner bitch. I wish I could
control this awful desire to lash out at them both and give them
a mouthful, but I can't. Crying makes me gasp for breath, so
I sit down on the bed, panting heavily.

'Mum?' Robbie comes in. 'Owen's coming home soon.' He
sits down and puts his arm round me. I know what he's saying.
Owen, my twenty-two-year-old baby, who feels he's already
missed time away at Uni.

'Please, Mum, it's only a machine.'

My sobs grow quieter.

'Please... please... Dad... we...'

Gareth stands awkwardly at the door. 'Lindy, please don't
do this to us.'

Their sad faces bring me back, hauling me in like a fish as
I follow them out.

'Well, I'll try it then,' I type. Back in the sitting room, Gareth
brings me a Baileys.

But I'm still not sure I want to. And, why didn't Professor
Handbag acknowledge my question?

Am I going to die soon, then?

And if I am, how soon is soon?

Two days later we're sitting in the Oncology Department at Chase Farm Hospital, waiting to see the wonderful Dr Scofield, Head of Palliative Care, who is so full of compassion and tenderness that as soon as she asks us to sit down, I all but collapse with emotion.

This wonderful woman is in fact a former registrar to my doctor brother, Viv. Some twelve years earlier, the two of them had co-written a paper called *The Management of Drooling* for people with degenerative, neurological illnesses. This seems bizarre and totally weird now that I am one of those people, and in the care of Viv's ex-colleague.

And then I ask the elephant question, the one no one really feels able or willing to answer given the unpredictability of MND and the subject of dying.

Slowly, and terribly gently, in the sweetest voice, she begins to give her professional opinion about the way my illness is progressing.

Chapter Eighteen

Keeping it in the Family

•

Horse poem

My beautiful silver horse is dead,
No longer can I stroke that noble head,
Or see his mighty profile standing proudly,
Or listen to the pounding of his hooves so loudly.

Never can I feel once more, his velvety muzzle
Gently sniff my hand when his mind was in a puzzle,
Or see his glorious, noble head reaching up high,
Now that he is way up in the sky.

How I loved my silver horse with a love I can't explain,
And wish for once my eyes could see him galloping
over the plain.

Lindy Lucas, aged 10

I was a quiet, shy, nervous little girl, not the sort of child you
would imagine growing up to teach in tough schools. When I
was five, I had been quite deeply troubled after my sister was
born by mum's Puerperal psychosis (a postnatal mental illness). This was closely followed by my best friend Katy's
leukaemia and subsequent death. Mum's despair and fright-
ening mood changes, as well as Katy's physically changed body
and different personality, had a great effect on me. People
could change – leave you – so instead I opted for animals and
threw myself into the loving reliable world of Perdy and the
rest of my pets. I dedicated myself completely to their physical
and emotional welfare which, as it turned out, was similar to
the way I later loved my own children.

So, my teaching career began with attempts to train and discipline various mice, rabbits, guinea pigs, Tara, the rat, and of course my loyal companion, Perdy, the mongrel, bought as a puppy from the local pet shop when I was seven. At eight, I started horse riding lessons where mastering control was paramount and these provided me with some of the necessary skills for my future life in the classroom.

My teenage diaries are detailed, full of angst and worries about not being pretty enough, but there is no evidence in them of an interest in wanting to teach. Mostly, they are full of me trying to understand myself – this deep analysing, I'm afraid, the legacy of growing up with a psychoanalyst for a father.

Insert a boy's name into the horse poem at the beginning of this chapter and already you can see the themes of suffering and lost love, which were to form the basis of my diaries for the next few years. However, no horse ever caused me the anguish that falling for unobtainable boys did. And as I got older, my horsey passion, although still alive and well, could not satisfy the desire for true love that years of reading *Jackie* magazine had given me. But being intense, over-sensitive and lacking in confidence did not bode well for romantic encounters with hormonally challenged fourteen-year-old boys.

Wuthering Heights, read and re-read throughout my adolescence, formed the basis of my search for 'the one'. Surely, it must only be a matter of time before a boy would '*look into my soul and love me for who I am.*' (Diary entry, 1971) Hah!

4th September 1969
I have been slipping back into depression ever since I discovered it's not fantastic and sheer heaven to have a boyfriend. When you long to have one and never have, one tends to transform it into some magical, romantic fixation; in love with a marvellous boy all starry eyes and happiness. But what a let down when you do actually manage to get one, it isn't really very pleasant, in fact a tie down and a bore.

The bore in question was a boy, let's call him, Jim, who went to a local school. We went out for a few months, though we only really went as far as our dining room, and then I got bored.

126

Poor Jim. According to my diary he: *had no opinions on things, typically working class, went to a secondary modern school and wasn't very intelligent.*

It gets worse. This was written after I had chucked him:

In fact, his sense of humour didn't exist. I like to be bossed around by the male, to a certain extent, to be the weaker protected female. Not to be the one who always had to make conversation first, and even when I did make a statement, it was always snubbed with, 'so' which wasn't really very encouraging. He hardly ever really spoke to me, never complimented me and, before I'd had a chance to open my mouth he'd remark 'What's up with you then?'

Cringe. So much for the Women's Lib of the 1970s. But my experience with Jim did not put me off my search for love.

Most of the time thoughts in my diaries were about various boys in my class or about how I was: *absolutely, bloody fed up and intolerant of all the stupid people around me*, whilst at the same time constantly comparing myself with slimmer, prettier, more academic girls; usually my two best friends.

My page-a-day diaries often started with: *Oh, God, I'm so depressed*, and later on, when I shared a flat with my gay friend, Steve (we were in our twenties), formed the basis of many a drunken reading session. After a few drinks in the local, we would stagger in and he'd say:

'Go on, Lindy, get the diaries out,' and we would howl and shriek with laughter until our stomachs ached.

Tom looked at me today whilst handing out the exercise book, maybe there is a chance for me if he breaks up with J.

C. and I got a bit queer on loads of cider. (Steve liked this one.)

Today a bird flew into the classroom and Mr Wilson was trying to help it escape. Everyone was laughing but I was nearly crying as I thought it might die. J and C were talking about how funny it was, the vile little sluts.'

I forgot to tell you that 'Bimbo' smiled at me in the shop this

127

morning when I was collecting my papers. He'll be nice when he's older.

Freaked out dancing To Led Zeppelin and Chicago at the School dance in my pink kaftan which everyone admired. I was going wild in my bare feet. The stroboscopic lighting was fantastic.

I feel so terrible I can't stand it, I want to die, oh, God, all I can do is cry I have been so deeply wounded. That one night with Roger will haunt me for a long time because now he avoids my eyes and does not speak to me.

Oh, if I can't get my job back in the paper shop, all my hopes and dreams of working with Sharkey again will be shattered and I'll have nothing and no one to live for.

'Stop a goddamn minute girl! For Christ's sake. I don't think I can take much more of this stuff, you've got three volumes of these godforsaken diaries. I think your readers get the message.'

A shrill voice over my shoulder, the finger tips pressing against my chest.

Mildred.

'Yes, you were a miserable self-obsessed teenager. So what? Come on, you need to get back to me. It's late now…' The weight on my chest increases as I feel her soft breath in my ear.

'Just a bit about school … about … about why I wanted to be a teacher…'

'Okay, but make it snappy girl, I tol' you, we ain't got all the time in the goddamn world.'

Secondary School, Finchley County Grammar

Looking back into the diaries kept in my school days, two things clearly stand out:

1. No teacher – despite my thin, miserable appearance during the months I went out with a rather strange troubled boy called Alan – ever asked me if I was all

right. This was something I remembered each time I noticed any child's unhappiness in my classes. At school I felt invisible but no one's misery ever passed me by once I was a teacher myself.

2. The boredom was unbelievable. The teaching was mainly copying from books, copying from the board or having notes dictated to us.

Actually, that was a bit of a lie about 'why I wanted to be a teacher'. The truth was I loathed school utterly and left at the end of the fifth year to do my A-levels at college. I had no intention of being a teacher, but poor A-level results after two years of partying left me little choice. All my friends and then boyfriend Bonny (Andrew Bonito) got places at university, a fact that deeply pissed me off, given their assorted habits of booze and drug dabbling. But, according to mum, getting a teacher-training certificate would open doors for the future.

Bonny and I took a gap year (not so fashionable then). I worked in Dolcis shoe shop, he at Hadley Wood golf course.

In 1974, Bonny got a place at Sussex University and I got a place at Teacher Training College in Brighton, though our two-year relationship ended a few months before we went.

The first term was spent with me wanting to leave. I'd made a mistake. I should be at university with like-minded intellectuals, not living in a women-only block full of god-squaddy bores who were all training to be primary school teachers.

But, like getting ill, suddenly, without any warning, my first experience of teaching gave me such an unexpected buzz that I fell in love. How had I never thought of it? The profession was perfect for me. I could be an actress, entertaining my classes, an intellectual passing on my passion for reading and writing, a social worker helping the wounded and the needy. It was never, ever going to be boring either. There was no way I was going to model myself on those idiotic fools in my grammar school, waddling around in their stupid crow-like gowns, putting you into rank order each summer because of your academic ability. No.

It was 1978. Education was changing. I had a Distinction in Teaching, a 2/1 B.Ed Hons and was in love with Irish Keith from Sussex University. We moved together to London, where I took up my first teaching position in a multi-cultural school in Neasden. This was the beginning of a thirty-two-year teaching career, which ended abruptly in 2010 with the diagnosis of Motor Neurone Disease.

Letter

•

This is from my dear friend, Jill Vonberg, who I met as Jill Smith many years ago, when we lived together in K Block at Brighton Polytechnic.

Dear Lindy,

I met you in September 1974. You had done a gap year and were 19 and I hadn't and was 18 and I felt rather immature compared to you.

On our first evening you had most of us on K block's ground floor (the 2nd floor was a different world) in to your room where we sat and exchanged names and details about ourselves. I remember in particular Jean Mountford who came from Doncaster and I was amazed that anyone lived so far away!

We got on from the beginning but I always felt impressed by you and therefore a little shy initially. You were very upright in your denim flares, clogs and a black and red striped rugby top with your long blonde hair hanging neatly down your back rather than flopping all over your face.

I remember meeting Jem and then you introducing me to Bonny and although Jem was good-looking, I could not imagine how you could have finished with such an utterly gorgeous boyfriend. Here was another reason to be impressed by you!

You seemed careful and controlled and I think that's why seeing you shuffle along the corridor to the bathroom in your lilac, quilted dressing gown with its inch of gold braid parallel to the edge, sticks in my mind. Your clogs off and no make-up made you look smaller and more vulnerable. I can see you now in your mule slippers with your sponge bag under your arm wearing that dressing gown, moving towards one of the bathrooms at the top of the corridor.

One evening a few of us met in Chris Bridgman's room with Charlie de Ledesma and I was further impressed because you knew how to roll a joint!

You were in a different education group from me and it seemed a lot more grown up and intellectual to be in the secondary one like you were. You were an avid reader and unlike me, you paced yourself when it came to written work and assignment deadlines.

You also paced yourself when it came to eating; I had a hearty appetite but you would stick to the same menu of grated cheese and coleslaw and the occasional jacket potato.

You invited me to stay in London with you and your family and I really enjoyed the happy atmosphere and was attracted to the whole family; I loved your Ted Hughes and Sylvia Plath parents and handsome Viv and sweet Karey who were still at school. In fact your Psychoanalyst father and Marie Stopes counsellor mother seemed slightly alternative and trendy!

You were the first person I'd met who could talk about feelings and I was fascinated about what you could discuss with your parents. You recognised I was depressed long before I did and you were incredibly supportive: making an appointment for me to see Dr Beynon, coming with me and encouraging me to seek counselling. This was probably a lifesaver. You always accepted me as I was and even when I withdrew into my own rather bleak world and I cut off contact with everyone, you were always there for me when I resurfaced.

131

Over the years our friendship has been consistent in that even when we haven't seen each other for ages, we pick up exactly where we left off when we meet up. Whatever our concerns have been over the years – which have included the men in our lives, marriage, (divorce and remarriage for me), children, teaching, weight gain, money, pensions, depression, counselling, our friends, parents, siblings, health and pets -- we have always been very interested in whatever each other has to say and without fail we have always had a really good laugh! You are a brilliant listener, endlessly sympathetic and you have a great sense of humour. I am still impressed by you!

With much love,
Your friend of 38 years,
Jill xx

Chapter Nineteen

The Ride of My Life

May 2012

•

I am going to die and I don't know how to bear it. What did I do wrong?

'Open your eyes, girl, for Pete's sake. What's the worst that can happen?'

A strong wind blows hair across my face but I keep my eyes shut. I'm gripping tightly onto a cold metal rail and I know by the voice, who I'm sitting next to.

'So you're gonna die like this, eh, without admiring the view first? Hun, I had you down as being made of much sterner stuff, but *c'est la vie* or in your case, *mort.*'

'Just shut the fuck up, Mildred – what the...?'

A juddering and clanking makes me open my eyes.

Jesus, oh, God, where the hell are we? I can't stand heights. Are we ... are we on like a big d... d... dipper?' I remember the terror of even watching 'The Pepsi Max Big One' in Blackpool, never mind being on it, and now... now... I squeeze my eyes back into a closed position.

'Journey to Oblivion' is the name kiddo, brand new ride as a matter of fact; it'll be the first time on it for both of us. And do try to watch your language, I'm afraid it's out of God's hands now.' Mildred moves closer to me.

'This is your moment hun, take it, or leave it. You got a little while to look back. Celebrate. Big yourself up about what you've achieved and don't even start with that old baloney about 'not much' or 'oh, no, I couldn't possibly'. You need to understand what it's been about now... well, you know...'

'But I'm not looking down, all right... just back.'

'That's my girl, just a sec I'll get us turned round.' A bit more clanging and juddering another blast of wind and then...

'You ready? Right then kid, open those goddamn eyes.'

The rollercoaster's tracks spread far into the distance, a graceful series of high points stretching out towards a clear blue sky.

'Fifty-six,' Mildred says, as if she knows I'm trying to count them. 'Your age.'

'I … I don't know…'

'Where to start? Well, not with your whole damn life story from zero to fifty-six, for sure. Think about some of the things you've had a passion for. Come on, you're supposed to be trying to look at your life from the full-bottle perspective – as in 'C' for Celebration. What would you like people to say about you at your funeral?'

'Stop stop, don't say that – '

'What the 'F' word? Sorry sweetie, but it's gonna happen whether you accept it or not. Think of this as an opportunity because, let's face it, you've not always been, how shall I say this, very good at enhancing the positives about yourself have you?'

Mildred sighs and begins filing her nails. The wind has gone, leaving a gentle breeze and the sun has emerged beaming down warm comforting rays onto my face.

'Just don't take all day kid, that's all.' Mildred takes out a pot of red nail-varnish and begins stroking the tiny brush over her perfectly shaped cuticles.

'I think I was quite successful as a teacher.'

'Cut the 'quite' out, please. Again…'

'I THINK I WAS A BRILLIANT AND INSPIRING TEACHER!' I shout, though Mildred chooses to ignore the sarcasm.

'Perfect,' she says fixing her yellow scarf more securely around her neck. 'Off you go then, you can start with that.'

Chapter Twenty

I Will Survive:

My First Year of Teaching

1978–1979

•

My career as a teacher began in a very tough school near Neasden and Dollis Hill Park, where some of the bodily remains of Dennis Nielson's killing spree were eventually discovered in the 1980s. There were a lot of excellent teachers, and despite it being a somewhat chaotic school, everyone was totally dedicated to the kids – as we were then allowed to refer to them. In those days, we did not merely see them as a level or a grade; they were young people from deprived backgrounds and everyone did their best to give them a decent education, including plenty of trips to the theatre and holidays abroad. Here are a few small snapshots of what it was like teaching in the late 70s. (Some names have been changed to protect the innocent.)

It's the start of my second week teaching at the William Gladstone High School, a comprehensive in the London Borough of Brent. I'm sitting in the staffroom next to fellow probationers, Jo and Nigel. Altogether there are twelve of us – fresh, keen and enthusiastic young teachers, bright-eyed and eager to immerse ourselves in our exciting new world of education. However, the previous week has been totally and crazily chaotic, and all my classes have been, to use that vile euphemism, 'challenging'.

'Good morning everyone, here is today's copy of the timetable.' Sidney Jenkins, the Deputy Head, stands lopsided – due to his bad leg – and waves a piece of paper in the air at the morning staff meeting. He tells us to take a copy from our pigeonhole and informs us that he is making progress with it, but it's all because of the new library. The building work, still incomplete, is apparently what has led to us roaming down corridors with our classes of unruly pupils, searching for our allocated rooms each day. You can feel the groans of frustration in the smoke-filled, coffee-saturated atmosphere as Ed Hughes, the Head, says:

'Mine's only a small one.' Then pauses to cough. Nigel elbows me in the ribs and I nudge him back and distract myself by studying the black marks on the scruffy beige carpet, then stubbing out my cigarette into the ashtray Jo and I are sharing.

'Just to thank you all for your understanding at the beginning of the new term and can you make sure that if Gidean DaCosta passes you with the stick I saw him with this morning, please take it off him.' Nigel nudges me again.

'Have a good day – yes, Miss Manning?' We all turn to look at the other Deputy Head – a short, plump figure with an odd pudding-basin haircut and sturdy, flat lace-ups – who is waving her arm about from the corner of the staffroom.

'You know she's fucking nuts, Lindy, don't you?' Nigel whispers. I bite back a terrible snort of laughter and manage to cough loudly instead.

'Morning, everyone, can I just remind you to check the girls' make-up. Anyone seen wearing any must be sent to me immediately, thank you.'

I'm not quite sure how she's going to fit several hundred girls into her office, but hey, I'm only concerned about getting my classes into a classroom – never mind the foundation and eyeliner.

It is 1978, and there are no computers to help with timetabling. Poor Sidney has to use pins with different-coloured heads, which he moves round on a huge board precariously balanced in his office. The board does actually fall off halfway through the following year.

Not only is the timetable unfinished, there are no schemes of work, no photocopiers or resources. Just a big banda machine in the staffroom where you can print off handwritten worksheets by rolling the master copy in ink and turning a handle, as if you were a Victorian scullery maid doing a week's laundry.

All we have in the English Department is *Stride Ahead in English* – books one-to-five and Ronald Ridout's books, one-to-five, plus piles of dusty classics, which I cannot imagine ever using with any of the classes I've taught so far. Maurice Phelps, the Head of English, has given only one piece of advice to Sue, Nigel and myself about teaching, and that is to, 'keep their heads down'.

He says these words almost every day, usually with a San Moritz cigarette balanced precariously in the corner of his mouth. He doesn't even take it out to inhale and quite often I stand mesmerised as the ash gets longer and longer, then sprinkling grey dust as it drifts towards the floor onto his dark suit. He has greased, shiny black hair and I seriously cannot remember anything much else he said to us. No one in his classes ever lifts their head up to speak.

Stride Ahead in English is comprised of exercises in which kids copy into their books the missing word. There are sentences such as, 'Mother takes the _____ from the oven.' and 'Father helps William play the _____ '

At the bottom of the page are the words they can choose. It is mindless, repetitive and involves little thinking. The kids love them, but this is not English teaching. It is unashamedly sexist and old fashioned. I cannot believe that this sort of rubbish passes for education.

'God, I hope I actually have a classroom for my fifth form. Yesterday, Sue and I were both lining up for the same room, it was a fucking nightmare,' I mutter to Jo as we head off up the long glass-corridor that connects the staffroom and offices to the rest of the school. 'Mind you, teaching in the English area is even worse as the sliding doors don't work,' I add.

Jo laughs and grips more firmly onto her two heavy bags. 'I'm really dreading my Y–3 bottom set, they were totally uncontrollable last week in the business studies room full of typewriters. They couldn't keep their hands off them! See you at break.' Jo turns into the foreign language department as the doors open and a scruffy bunch of Year 5s push past us.

'Hi, Miss, we got you today?' Jonny, a thin white boy, stands in front of me. He's in my Y–4 bottom set, and is obviously completely mad. He twitches awkwardly and pulls a sheet of crumpled paper out of his blazer pocket.

'Here's my homework, Miss.' He stuffs it into my hand and scuttles off before I have a chance to thank him.

In my classroom, I dump my two bags down and unfold the paper.

My nam is jonny. I lik firs [Fires he means] I cant right wel. I hav a cat.

(He tries to burn the school down eighteen months later.)

Poor Jonny, how am I ever going to get him to pass an exam in two years' time?

I sit down at my desk and open up a large green register, already a mess of black lines and red circles, which I'm worried I'll be told off about by Jenny, the scary Head of First Year, as I keep filling in the wrong days. However, I manage to savour the last few minutes of peace just before a head pops round the door.

'Can we come in, Miss?'

The 1 LL (1 Lindy Lucas' class) stream into the room as I begin my morning battle for order.

At some point in the year, Ed begins bringing his dogs into school, two longhaired mongrels that loll about in his office all day. Mrs O'Leary, his loyal secretary, a short, plump motherly woman, has been heard muttering about these dogs that leap out of Ed's car every morning. A shocking rumour is flying around that she has even aimed a sly kick at one of them. Tyrone, a tiny black boy who doesn't know what his surname is, often takes the dogs for walks in Gladstone Park when he finds himself sent out of lessons and ends up sitting outside Ed's office. One morning I find Ed washing one of the dogs in front of the school and am asked by him if I've ever smelt a dead squirrel because this was why Simba was having a bath.

'Er... no... I haven't,' I reply, sidling past Simba's huge, soapy body and slavering chops.

Al Davies, a large, loud Welshman, complains in the staffroom that the dogs leap up and sniff his crotch whenever he goes into Ed's office. But no one dares say anything because, after all, Ed is the Head.

Ed has also become obsessed with attracting birds to the school and has ordered the caretaker to put bird boxes up in as many places as possible, whilst ignoring that even in lesson time, the corridors are full of kids who are bunking off lessons. (The following year he interrupts an A-level lesson so that he can look at the Cole Tits nesting outside my classroom window. My sixth formers had thought he had been asking if my tits were cold, they informed me afterwards, when we had all stopped crying with laughter.)

Teaching is very, very tough. I go home to Keith in the evenings, frequently sobbing and then drinking too much, as I recount my frequent disastrous lessons. Controlling these streetwise teenagers is a challenge I'm not sure I'm up to. I spend hours preparing interesting lessons, writing out worksheets, marking exercise books and telling Keith that I'm no good.

'Of course you are,' he assures me constantly in his calm voice, 'give it time.' He has faith in me, but I am wracked with self-doubt and insecurity, forever trying to set boundaries for behaviour which my pupils always manage to trample down.

In the summer term I have a visit from the English advisor, Moira Bolton, to judge if I am going to pass my probationary year. She's going to come and see me with the Y–4 bottom-set, the one with Jonny in it and another six variously illiterate, dysfunctional kids.

'Oh, God, Keith, I'm going to fail,' I cry to him the night before, over a glass of wine.

'Listen, Lindy, you're not. Right? You're a really good teacher, I've seen how hard you work, honestly, you're too hard on yourself.' He puts his arm round me.

Keith always makes me feel better but I'm terrified the kids will deliberately mess around because someone else is in the room.

I can't remember what the lesson was about but at some point during it, the film *The Exorcist* is seized on by Billy Metcalf to make a point (God knows what) and then, in the next moment, he stands up, lies back on a desk, and pretends to masturbate with an imaginary crucifix.

If there had been a cupboard nearby I might have dived into it, but there is nowhere to hide and I have no choice but to stand, pale and motionless, as Billy writhes around making what he thinks are the sounds of someone in ecstasy. Jonny has gone even paler, biting his pencil nervously whilst Dipak, Carly, Jess and Tyrone are sitting with their mouths open, completely shocked at Billy's outrageous behaviour.

'Billy, Billy, this is not acceptable,' I tell him, though noticing a pathetic hint of pleading in my voice. Moira Bolton is noisily turning the page of her large, black folder as the knot of panic turns into a cannonball.

'But, Miss, she 'ad the devil in 'er,' Billy grins, glancing over at Moira. Little shit, I think, suddenly realising he's doing this on purpose.

'Enough, Billy!' I roar, surprised by the new assertive quality in my voice.

Moira's head bobs up, down, up, then down again, reminding me of a chicken as the pen scratches menacingly across her folder.

'Sit down, stop misbehaving and let's get on with the lesson.' I point at his chair, daring him to defy me. He slithers grudgingly off the desk and slumps back into his seat.

'I love Miss Lucas' lessons,' says Carly loyally, looking at Moira. A faint smile makes her mouth twitch very slightly and Carly beams at me. Dear girl.

After they have gone, Moira acknowledges what a diverse and difficult group they are, but tells me it is obvious they all respect me and that they have made some progress this year. Really? I think, but I don't say anything. I pass! Thank God.

'I can't believe I have survived,' I tell Keith that evening in the posh French restaurant where we go to celebrate, a joint celebration I recall, as he had just been promoted at work.

'See, I told you,' he says, grinning as we put our glasses of wine together with youthful optimism.

Sadly, we break up six months later. I stay at William Gladstone for another nine years.

Letter

•

This is from my friend, Jo Rex, from William Gladstone.

Dear Lindy

You asked me to write down my first impressions of meeting you, so here goes…

I can't recall what I first thought when I met you but I remember that whole period at William Gladstone and the people we met and worked with. All those probationers – it seemed at times as if the whole school was run by young probationary teachers! Nigel, Sue R, Ted, Robina (Rowena – funny woman!!), Howard, you, me and others whose names I have now forgotten.

We were so young and that made it such a fun place to be – we all struggled together and tried hard to become teachers and we had a really good time together. It was chaos – the staff room just a mess of piles of exercise books, worksheets, wads of paper – and the coffee and fags. All so exciting when you are 24 and armed with all your plans for injecting new life into the teaching profession!! And we were presided over by Mr Mort who looked just like Vidal Sassoon!

I got married in the first half term of William Gladstone but that didn't seem to impact on life at WGHS apart from having to change my name from Miss Owens to Mrs Rex. I had tried to keep my own name at the school but this proved too much for Eric Sheldon and that weird timetable board he had with loads of little pins sticking in it. Being young I acquiesced and changed my name – hope I wouldn't do that today!!

In all this you were my special friend – the person who was learning with me and battling against the odds at times with difficult kids just as I was. Oh those students – Rodney, Jerome, Ken, Claudette, Sharon, Donna to name but a few. Looking back on it, I realise how hard it was and certainly how inadequate some of my lessons were. You and I would bemoan the times when something we thought would work just hadn't and we would always feel pissed off that Sue R never seemed to get a hair out of place or looked flustered – as you and I regularly did!! But you, Nigel and I could see the funny side of it and always managed to have a laugh.

And indeed, you, Nigel and I were soon under the spell of Scilla and the infamous Literature and Society course – or L&S as we called it. Oh, my God, the hours you and I spent carping about Scilla whom we admired and feared in roughly equal measure. She used to reduce us to gibbering wrecks at times since we could never really match up to her expectations and demands - but it was so exciting, nevertheless, when we would go to meetings at her flat and discuss all manner of issues both political and literary. If I am honest, there were times when I just felt totally out of my depth but it was still a brilliant time. And she taught us loads.

So that is the context within which you and I got to know each other and in those two years other people filled out the background – Dennis, Dave, Sue B, Charlotte, Brian, Ian, Cheryl, Norelle... Where are they now?

You were scatty and panicky – always a bit of a drama queen in those days with a dangerous streak. To a young woman who had been brought up in a working-class family in South Wales – a rather dysfunctional family to use common parlance – you were a glimpse of another world and other possibilities. I envied you your lovely family and big house and your reckless life in Brighton and all your stories. You were just fun to be with and only later did I come to understand how painful some of those stories really were.

As we began to learn more about each other and talk about our families and the men we had loved and went on to love we also started to see into each other's inner selves and expressed those doubts and the sadness that ran throughout our lives right up to today. I had never met anyone who had counselling and was fascinated by it but I was always alarmed at the way in which you embarked upon relationships that should have had large warning signs written all over them. Oh the hours we spent over bottles of wine spilling out all our stories.

That's one of my biggest memories of those days with you in William Gladstone – talking loads over bottles of wine, smoking packets of cigarettes, getting far too drunk and then trying to get into work the next day. And having to get to the end of the teaching day before we could catch up on our sleep. There was one evening when you and Sue R and I got totally drunk and couldn't get to work the next day – so we all rang in with lame excuses as to why we couldn't make it in. Presumably somebody must have thought it strange that we were all ill on the same day!

As I write this I think the word I would use to describe you at the beginning of our friendship is colourful. You wore bright clothes, long, dangly earrings and you laughed a lot – quite a loud and distinctive laugh. And I know that you doubted your ability to be a good teacher whom kids would respect – which has of course proven to be utter nonsense! You always say that you admired my ability to be a disciplinarian with my classes – it was all an act really. And, of course, of the two of us you are the one who stayed the course and helped all those students to greater things – as witnessed by all the shows of affection you continue to receive from them.

So you overcame your doubts and became a confident teacher who used a love of books and literature to enrich other people's lives. And you continue to be colourful and when we meet now in circumstances that are sometimes so painful and poignant that I can't find the language to describe how I feel you are still colourful – the way you dress and the way you tap away on your iPad enable all that colour to display itself. And when you tap I can hear you laugh.

There was no good reason why we lost contact from about 2005 –it just happened. But when we met again af-

143

ter Mildred came calling, those years just melted away
and we have just picked up the thread and continued the
story.

With much love

Jo xxx

*Ah yes, my reckless streak and the relationship that should have
had a warning sign. This was when I discovered that what I thought
was a green field was actually a pool of slime.*

Chapter Twenty-One

Edmonton County:

The Best and Worst of Times

1998–2005

•

Dear Miss Jones,

Thank you for all your help and support over the last two years! Your lessons have been entertaining, your a joka miss!

Lots of love,
Emma

To Mrs Jones,
Thank you for everything. You have been the best teacher I've ever had, and the funniest.
I will try my hardest to read more books.

Love you,
Kaley

Words inside cards from two Year-11 girls.
(Obviously, Emma was away during my spelling and grammar lessons.)

'Seems like you got through to those girls, sweetie.' Mildred looks up from filing her nails and smiles.

'Yes, but they drove me crazy too,' I say remembering how they giggled and distracted each other during lessons.

'But listen, you can't write about every school you've ever worked in. You can pick one more, all right?'

'Edmonton County.'

'Off you go then, but…'

'Yeah, yeah … don't go on for too long.'

'That's my girl.'

I joined the school in April 1998, as Deputy Head of English. At that time there were two separate sites: the Lower School and the Upper School. Despite, or possibly because of, the madness of the constant travelling of teachers between them, both staffrooms were entertaining places to be in.

I can still remember driving across the A10 at break, arriving in the staffroom for either a few quick sips of coffee or a mad dash to the loo, then fighting my way through the overcrowded corridors, often with two bags, to teach and then possibly having to drive back to the other site at lunchtime. It was totally manic, but a great excuse when you hadn't finished your marking because you had left it at the Upper/Lower School, depending on where you were.

I was based at the Upper School and was next to Stuart, the Head of Modern Languages, who had a very loud voice, a raucous laugh and had me in stitches whenever he described meetings with his line manager about 'Embedding New Initiatives'. He could give you a long list of other kinds of bullshit words that he detested and would tell them to me whenever he found a particularly pretentious one. Trying to work in that staffroom was almost impossible. I laughed a lot and far too loudly.

On my first day there I was nervously expecting the unsuccessful internal candidate, Mike, to be ready to hate my guts. But his first words to me were ones of admiration that I had managed to teach an extremely long, wordy poem called 'Nutting' by Wordsworth in my previous school that had been much less academic.

'I mean, how the hell did you do it?' he asked.

'I acted it out,' I told him. 'I danced down an imaginary country lane and then gasped in amazement that I had found a few nuts growing on some bushes.'

Mike's outburst of laughter sealed our friendship and was the start of a lot of serious giggling between the two of us over the next few years.

Pete, my Head of Department, informed me that one of the

reasons I had been given the job was so that I could tidy up Mike's desk, but seemed totally oblivious to the fact that his was equally, if not more, chaotic.

What worried me most though was the rumour that he'd left a rotting cucumber from a sex education lesson underneath a pile of marking for six whole humid weeks of the summer holidays. I mean, what sort of place had I come to? I later discovered that the miscreant was Elaine. She was the one who'd accidentally left it on Pete's desk at the end of a frenetic summer term, where it had festered away, discarding its stinking skin onto a pile of Year-7 poems. (I hadn't, at this stage, realised that travelling between two sites during break and lunch inevitably turned you into a disorganised, untidy wreck.)

Attempting to spruce up my dull-looking classroom, I asked Pete for some bright paper and felt tips. There was no paper left, he apologised, but he did have some felt-tips. The scruffy little box he handed me was seriously disappointing: half of the felt-tips were completely dried up while the rest had the wrong colour lids on. Then Pete handed over a fat, juicy stationery catalogue and told me to order whatever I liked. It was love at first sight. Perusing the pages of *Educational Supplies* thus became one of the favourite parts of my role. I was in heaven, browsing through pages and pages of goodies and never got over the thrill of being able to decide which shade of sugar paper I could purchase. And I mean you can never have too many packets of luminous Post-it notes, sticky, gold stars or rainbow-coloured display paper, can you?

The following scenes will hopefully capture something of these times and reveal the way I was before I became ill.

Scene One: A Sixth Form Tutorial – 2004

c

By this time I was now the permanent Head of English.

'Now everyone, we have to plan out what we, 12JNL, are going to do as a form, for the old-folks party in December.'

I am trying my best to sound enthusiastic but I can't think of anything worse than having to help them plan out dance routines/singing/etc. Some of the old folk had nearly fainted the previous year when, as they knocked back glasses of sherry, some half-naked girls gyrated provocatively on chairs in front of them. Roger, the Head of sixth form, has given strict orders that it must be wholesome entertainment, but Tara and Katie still want to do something from *Chicago*.

'Definitely not. Come on everyone, what shall we do?'

Steve arrives a little late and sits down.

'Sorry, Jones, woke up late, where's *Tricia*?' he asks, looking at the television, which is noticeably silent.

'Steve, we don't always watch *Tricia* in tutorials,' I say indignantly, trying to keep a straight face because, let's face it, an hour a week on topics such as, "How to eat healthily,' are pretty uninspiring compared to a slanging match on *Tricia*.

'Yes, we do, Miss, when you can't be bothered to do the set stuff with us.' Jerome grins.

'I certainly don't. Anyway, Steve, any ideas for the old folks?'

'Carol singing?'

'Brilliant. Right everyone, what carols do you know?'

The door opens and my friend, Viv, pops her head round the door. 'Blimey, you've got a lot of kids. Have we got assembly this morning?' she asks.

'No,' says the annoying Jerome smugly.

'Er, yes, we have,' I tell her rolling my eyes. 'We're practising our carol singing,' I say as the television bursts into life. 'For the old folks.'

'Such a drag,' she whispers as she shuts the door.

'She's well out of order, that woman,' Sophie shouts.

'Excuse me, Ms Franzmann is a colleague not...'

'No, Miss, this woman on *Trisha*, she's been shagging her best friend's ... oy, Chris, get off my...'

'Turn that tele off, for...'

'Jones, sorry, gotta see Miss Taylor about my coursework, but don't forget my tutorial tomorrow in E67.' Steve grins and pretends to sing into an imaginary microphone, 'While shepherds wash their socks by night...'

'Yes, thank you, Steve. Right now, who knows the words to 'Silent Night', we...'

A shrill bell rings out as we all look at each other for a second.

'Fire alarm! Hurrah! No assembly!' shouts Tara, as they all suddenly come to life. We head out into the playground and I meet Viv on the way with the five members of her tutor group.

'I just can't be arsed with this old-folks stuff can you?' She says, as we clutch our registers.

'Nah, me neither, but at least today I don't have to chase them round the art block. It pisses me right off, the way they run away each week whenever we have assembly.'

We reach the sixth-form fire-drill assembly point where a motley assortment of students is noisily snaking into four uneven lines.

'Ah, Ms Jones, I'll need your list of group activities by tomorrow, okay?'

'Sure Roger,' I say confidently as the skies open to a mass groan.

Scene Two: She Who Must Be Obeyed

·

Its 9.30 on a Monday morning and Year 11 are still more or less asleep. We have been 'doing a poem' for the last half-hour, although I think 'we' is a slight exaggeration. I have been dancing around in front of my colourful PowerPoint, attempting to persuade 'the learners' to at least pretend they are interested.

'Oh, no, why is it always poems?' Glen asks at the start of the lesson, slumping down on his desk and putting his coat over his head. A stern reminder from me about the classroom rules mean that his coat is now on his chair, but when I stroll purposefully over to him, his exercise book is blank.

Talking to him in my 'positive and encouraging' teacher voice, I manage to get him to hold his pen in his hand before I'm interrupted by the sound of rustling paper. I turn round to see that Keely has lined up a roll, three sandwiches, a bag of crisps and a drink on top of her anthology.

'Er, Keely, what are you doing?'

'Miss, it's breakfast, I ain't had nuffink to eat. I have to get up at five to do me 'air.'

The hair in question is scraped back off her face so tightly her eyes are slightly slanted. Perfect curls are pressed decoratively around her cheekbones and forehead, flattened with hairspray – or possibly gel – into her pale skin.

'See,' she points at a curl, 'that takes ages, man.'

'Please don't call me 'man', Keely, and put away your food, thank you, this is an English lesson.' I start to pull out an incident slip as she takes a bite out of her egg sandwich.

'All right, all right, I'm putting my stuff away, all right?'

'Thank you, Keely,' I say as she noisily shoves everything back into her bag. I feel quite pleased with my success today. The advice from the Behaviour Management Consultant seems to have worked:

'"Please" sounds like begging. Always follow an order with "thank you", and increase your power by using a student's name.'

Keely glares at me, brushing crumbs onto the floor as I return to the front.

Ten minutes later, I think we have made some progress. I remind them again about the rule of always backing up your point with evidence in the form of a quotation when...

'Miss, what's that noise?' says Andy.

I look over at Keely who has an oblong thing on her desk which is – oh, God – is it a vibrator?

'Keely?'

'Wot?'

'The... that... um... on your desk?' Everyone has now turned round to look.

'You mean me nail file?' She says switching it on and running it over her chosen finger.

'It's good. Miss, do you wanna go?'

Thankfully, the bell rings at this point.

•

'Oy, Mrs Jones, keep the noise down there's far too much fun going on in here.' Sandy pops her head round the door to the English Office.

'Working hard as usual, I see. Got any sweets?' She scoops a handful from the pot. It's Friday and I always take some in. Sandy is an honorary member of our department because she likes the way we try our hardest with everyone, even the ones who drive us crazy. She runs the Learning Centre, working with students who have been referred there due to poor behaviour.

'Any chance of some sweets, Jones? Mr Arto said we could have some.' Steve and Sophie appear next to Sandy, two of my sixth form who constantly tease me about a Mr Tom Arto who I told them taught French at the Lower School when Sophie asked me if I knew who Mr Tom Arto was. (Tomato joke, which I fell right into, in case you're having trouble.)

•

I spent seven happy years at Edmonton, but then, in March 2005, I had an accusation of assault made against me and everything changed.

It started on an ordinary Monday afternoon in March. I had left my A-level group for a few minutes so that I could help clear the corridors. There was a great crush of pupils making their way to their first lesson after lunch, and there were also mutterings about a fight. I stood at the corner with my arm out, telling students to turn back and go the other way. Suddenly, a boy I had taught two years previously, decided that he was going to go down it anyway, regardless of some old teacher.

I asked him politely to turn back but instead he called me a retard, pushed me on my shoulders and barged past me to get to his classroom. Shocked by this aggression, I swore and instinctively pushed him away from me before breaking down in tears and stumbling off to the staffroom.

Later on, in a meeting between us, the boy apologised, acknowledging that he had lost his temper, and I apologised for swearing. As far as we were concerned, the matter was finished, but not to his mother. Known to the school for her aggressive behaviour, she then marched her son off to the police station to lodge an assault charge against me. (Although apparently, the boy told the police he didn't want anything to happen to me.)

Meanwhile, students were busy writing in their statements that I had pushed him first. I was devastated. If this happened now, I would be suspended immediately, but the Head totally supported me, and so I was allowed to stay at work even though my name had now been given to Child Protection. In the world of teaching it is the child's word against yours, and if they want to lie, en masse, you are, without a doubt, totally powerless.

But of course, I now had to be interviewed by the police and when I was told that the boy had a red mark on his wrist where I had grabbed him, I simply collapsed. The whole thing was a nightmare. How could this be happening, I kept asking myself? My union solicitor was excellent and constantly tried to reassure me that it would not get to court, which of course it didn't, but pupils would come and ask me why I hadn't been suspended, which I found very distressing.

Two terrible weeks passed as I waited for the police's decision as to whether they were going to charge me . The CCTV camera showed the boy laughing and joking seconds after supposedly being attacked by me, so the police decided there was not enough evidence. But his mother was determined to carry on with her campaign against me (even though she had never attended parents' evenings when I'd taught her son).

She wrote a long letter to the Head alleging that I was amongst other things, a liar, mentally ill and had launched an unprovoked physical attack on her son by attempting to scratch his eyes out. (I am 5' 3"; the boy in question was much taller.) Even though anyone reading this one-sided rant against me would come to the conclusion that she was the one with serious mental health issues, I crumbled under the strain and felt I had to leave, although her vicious attempt to get me sacked had brought no repercussions on her at all.

The Head warned me that she might try to take out a private prosecution against me, so I spent the next four months in a state of terrible anxiety. At this point, Gareth was so angry he was all for trying to get her charged with defamation of character, but we were advised against this.

I found another job as Head of English at Cheshunt School and my friend, Viv, incensed by what had happened to me, began to research the subject of false allegations made against teachers. This eventually resulted in her award-winning play, *Mogadishu*. So something very good came out it, but it had been a terrible ordeal and had completely shattered my confidence.

'That was tough, kid, being accused like that.' Mildred is staring straight at me.

'Yes... yes... it was terrible,' I mutter. 'I'd been so happy there that's why it hurt so much... I mean, one of the students who gave a statement was a girl I'd taught, who'd been in the same English class as the boy... I just couldn't get my head round her betrayal. Perhaps it was a bit of a laugh for her... or maybe she liked him or something... but it nearly ruined my career when I'd worked so hard... been so committed. '

'Lots of them will remember you, sweetie, and not because of that bad stuff.'

'Yes, I guess so,' I say sadly, 'despite all that, I miss teaching terribly and why the hell am I writing about this when I'm meant to be celebrating?'

'Well, you survived, kid, you kept right on going, that takes guts.'

'Hmm, maybe...'

'Just think of the ones you helped.' Mildred pats my shoulder. 'There are a lot more of them than that boy and his crazy mother.'

'I know,' I sniff.

But it doesn't make dying any easier.

Chapter Twenty-Two

Living Days

July 2012

•

'Is that it then? Celebrations over?' Mildred shivers and looks
up at the darkening sky. Clouds are now drifting towards us
and the sun is starting to sink.
  'I don't know what else... I mean... my sons?'
  'Goes without saying, kiddo; two great young guys.' Mildred
puts her jacket on as a cool breeze embraces us.
  'Well, if you don't mind me butting in, I've got to thinking
how hard you persevere... I mean you've put so much of yourself into so many different things. You spent time trying to help
your students... talking to them... preparing lessons... caring
for your sons... reading all those novels... and the way your
friends and ex-pupils keep wanting to see you – goddamit –
all the effort you've put in... and your writing! Years and years
of writing... going on courses... submitting novels... getting
knocked back. And yet here you are in your dying days still
tapping away, though, hell, the one-fingered typing does my
head in.'
  'Yes, yes, I packed a lot in, didn't I?'
  'And we haven't even started on the holidays, the theatre,
concerts and films... the book club...'
  'And all the stuff I've done since you came into my life.'
  'Girl, you've done me proud. I mean you joined two writing
groups last year, and even did a little teaching with Sandy and
and her dog, Google. That was just great, hun, especially the
way you went back into a school, which I know you found
hard and even though your speech was...'
  'Going.'
  'Precisely.'
  'What I'm trying to say here, Lindy, is that you're not a quit-
ter.'

The carriage sways gently and I feel intensely how very much I have loved life, despite its difficulties. I have fought so hard during the last 22 months, trying to cram as much as possible into each day, not wanting to waste my precious time.

According to what the lovely Dr Scofield had told me in May, I'm unlikely to have much more than another year, 'roughly' (as opposed to smoothly, which sounds much more comforting and definite). A year is nothing. I can hold a year in my hand – a thick, Smith's page-a-day diary. But then again, it's better than days or weeks.

'I... I... don't know... what to write about next... I...'

Mildred leans forward and puts her hand gently onto my arm. 'Whatever you want, kiddo, it's your book, just let me know when you've finished because...' We both look into the bright, orange glow sweeping across the clouds.

'I know.'

•

My good friend, Scary Sandy, was once asked by a student if she was a racist.

She glared down at her and replied:

'No, I just hate everyone equally.'

Enough said.

Outwardly, she's cynical, tough and outspoken and was the only person at Edmonton County who commanded the respect of the most belligerent and argumentative little cherubs.

We'd always had a great laugh together at Edmonton and her leaving gift to me in 2005 was to kidnap the English Department mascots, two Fluffalumps who were used periodically by us as teaching aids. Photographs of these poor teddy-like creatures appeared in the Friday bulletin for six weeks, photographed with various captions such as:

'Help we have been moved. We think we are in a dungeon somewhere. Now nobody will find us ... (not that anyone is looking for us).' You get the idea.

Anyway, she has a beautiful Golden Retriever called Google, who was raised to be an assistance dog, but failed to qualify on the grounds that his dandruff made him unusable. He is extremely well-trained, calm and gentle.

Sandy works in behaviour support for Enfield Council, going into schools to help students who are on the verge of being permanently excluded. She started using Google to help in their exploration of the issues of trust, respect and learning.

Just after Christmas, she asked me to write a lesson plan around Google, which would be used in a Year–7 class with poor literacy skills. The lessons were all written as if Google were speaking, and structured in such a way that the last two sessions would involve students writing a simple story around Google and his friends, Taggy, Duffy and Scrappy.

'So, everyone, last week we talked about what Google looked like, can you remember?'

'Miss, we said his eyes were like two chocolate buttons which is simlees,' a small, scruffy boy answered proudly.

'Well done, Omar, that was good. Can everyone remember what a simile is?' Sandy invites other responses. I move the lesson on.

'Now this week we're going to think about his personality. Can you tell what someone's like by what they look like?'

'Yes, Miss,'

'No, Miss, 'cos there's a Staffie on our estate and he looks fierce but he's not…'

Discussion builds around the topic as Google wanders round the students, stopping by each one so that they can stroke him. One boy is initially petrified but, as Sandy points out, trust needs to be worked on, so she allows the boy to keep the distance he feels he needs.

Just being in the presence of such a calm dog makes everyone, including me, feel, well, blessed. Google definitely exudes some sort of transformative power. Watching him interact with damaged young people is amazing – they genuinely seem to believe he is really speaking to them.

Students read their work out to Google and listen attentively to his weekly diaries, whilst he shows them how he can read.

They love it. Even the most challenging students soon become besotted with Google the Wonder Dog.

Sandy and I run two sessions in a secondary school and one with Year-5 in a primary school for students identified with behaviour issues. Alison, the class teacher, leads the sessions, and Sandy, Google and myself all join in.

'Oh, Miss, Sandy, can Google really read?'

'Yes, of course, and he can take my socks off, look, here Google,' Sandy uses her clicker and holds out her foot. Google pulls gently at the sock.

'Oh, Miss, that's so cool, he's really smart, ain't he Miss?'

'I love learning with Google here.'

It is a bittersweet time.

Now I am the lady 'who can't speak proper', according to Jenny, a girl I have to do a lesson observation on. It was a science lesson and Jenny kept staring over at me. After informing me about my speech, she asked me if I could read and write! I had to laugh.

By January 2012, my speech had deteriorated further and I didn't feel I could cope going into schools anymore. Sandy is still doing the same work and only last Friday brought some students' writing to show me. Again, pleasure and sadness – such is my life now.

It occurred to me the other day, typing my Visa card details into an order form, that my card is going to outlive me. Expiry date: May 2015. But it's still impossible to think of, really imagine myself, vanishing.

In morbid introspective moments, I think about my absence from the house I have lived in for 25 years. How is it possible that I may not be here next year?

Robbie and Owen call me 'the finder' because I always manage to locate lost things. Robbie even managed to joke once about holding a séance in the future to ask me where something was. More dramatically, I imagine myself like the ghost of Catherine Earnshaw in *Wuthering Heights*, clawing at the window, begging to be let back in. But in some ways it's as if I'm already trapped outside, not really part of the world anymore.

Now, totally unable to talk, I have to rely on my right hand to type everything onto my iPad and the effort of writing, even the most trivial things, means that my temper tantrums and crying fits of frustration are becoming more frequent. This is especially so with the difficulties I am now having getting

dressed, not to mention Gareth's impatience with my compli-
cated clothes.

'That's a fucking sleeve,' I type furiously onto my iPad, as
my head is wedged into a small gap of material. And don't get
me started on his attempts to put my hat on. Since when did
he think that making me look like Benny Hill was acceptable?
Sorry, Gareth, I know you are trying your best...

Food is out, too. Gone. Funny to think that I'll never eat another meal. Being in a crowded Wetherspoons surrounded by
people stuffing their faces and knocking back booze can reduce
me to despair. I feel like those starving people in days of old
who were tortured by being suspended in hanging baskets
over banquet tables.

At home one evening last week, the smell of sausages and
bacon was so overwhelming that I found myself guiltily lifting
the sausage off Gareth's plate and sniffing its juicy, succulent
skin. Oh, to scoff down a bacon sandwich smothered in tomato
ketchup!

'Stop it for Pete's sake! Think of your readers. Come on,
you're supposed to be trying to lift their spirits. Where's that
Lindy who's trying to live like a butterfly?' Mildred appears
next to me.

'It's her day off, it's the turn of miserable old caterpillar, and
she wants to spend it rolling around in the dirt and crying.
Aren't I entitled to some good wholesome bitterness?'

'At least you're not actually a caterpillar, bedbound or totally
paralysed are you?'

'No, but I want to feel sorry for myself – and stop interrupting me – you said this was my book so...'

'Point taken.'

The rant of self-pity continues.

And the house is cluttered with bottles of liquid food sup-
plements and machines which keep me alive. We have:

1. The suction machine, for getting rid of excess saliva.
2. The Bipap – Hannibal Lecter breathing mask. (Non-
   invasive breathing ventilator.)
3. The pump for overnight PEG feeding.

4. Six boxes of Ensure TwoCal drinks to syringe into my feeding tube. Yum.
5. A box of syringes to pump this Ensure into myself, three times a day via my PEG. (Works with vodka, too, I discovered.)
6. A box of overnight feeding goo, plus packets of plastic piping.
7. A tin of Thick and Easy – a powder to make drinks thicker, thus easier to swallow. (What a great name, eh?)

And the air is thick with my anger.

'Why do you have to buy these massive bottles of shampoo?' I type, stalking into the kitchen. 'I can't fucking lift them with my weak arms!' I'm surprised the force of my typing finger hasn't pressed right through the iPad.

'Don't get so angry!' shouts Gareth, 'Robbie chose them.' (They do the shopping together now, I cannot cope with supermarkets.)

'And the milk, look.' I reach out for the massive six-pint carrier and try to lift it. The tops of my arms are now so weak any kind of movement which involves raising them is hopeless. Pressing on the shower button needs two arms; my stronger left one to lift the weak pathetic right one up. Make-up needs two hands and the other day, for the first time, I could not manage to put deodorant on and had to ask for help.

'Why doesn't anyone understand how hard things are getting for me?' I type, bursting into tears.

'Sorry, all right, sorry.'

I e-mail the doctors on Monday and, as usual, ask them to fax over the prescription for the specially made up and very expensive dribble medication. And, as usual, it doesn't arrive. The chemist, however, feels he now has to write things down even though he's known me for years.

It's not here yet, he writes.

More noisy sobbing.

But he's kind. He rings the surgery and he says he'll order it for me anyway as it takes a day or two to make it up.

I feel so helpless, I type. He nods sympathetically.

I go home to an empty house and lie crying on the sofa, even Scrappy ignores me, despite my calls of 'Ap, Ap', – I'm unable to pronounce his name properly anymore. He lies on the rug in the hall with his eyes shut, wagging his tail only slightly when I get up to see where he is. If I pour a glass of Baileys, he'll soon be by my side, eager to get his long, greedy tongue into it, I think bitterly, flopping back onto the sofa and checking my e-mails for about the 20th time. Nothing. No texts, either.

Everyone's forgotten about me, I think, snot and tears covering the cushion. I cry harder.

And the hole in my stomach, where the plastic tube comes out, is still sore despite efforts by the district nurse to sort out the over-granulation. (Read – scabby, bulging, sore.)

I remember Molly telling me that these are my living days. Huh? I tell myself again this is just one old stupid, grey, boring wet Wednesday. But it doesn't help.

It's too late to be up writing, alone in my small, cluttered workroom where I must have, in my previous life, spent months, if not years, marking essays and planning lessons. Outside, the night carries its own secrets but here, now, keys click in the front door. And inside, my family all noisily home now, are three deep voices bantering in the corridor by the kitchen about their chest hair, or lack of it.

Downstairs, Owen is telling Gareth and Robbie how Squeaky pissed in the black bin-bag in his room. Gareth asks me if that brown gunk he'd covered with toilet paper at the top of the stairs was actually cat crap. 'Yesh,' I tell him, as Robbie informs us again about how badly the leather sofa has started to stink of cat wee. Meanwhile, Scrappy runs around us all carrying his rabbit, whilst Squeaky appears, yowling for food at the top of the stairs. We can't help laughing.

In the midst of life, we are in death. Likewise, in the midst of tragedy, we find ourselves in the middle of inexplicably comic moments in our ordinary little lives.

'Night, Beaky,' says Robbie.

'Night, Mum,' says Owen.

My two precious boys, how hard it is to leave you.

Chapter Twenty-Three

Me and Mrs Jones

July 2012

•

The next day turned out to be an unexpectedly brilliant one. My friend Jo and I go back to 1978. We met at the William Gladstone High School where I was Miss Lucas and she was Miss Owens and we were starting our teaching careers together. Anyway, 34 years later, we are sitting in a quiet bar in Muswell Hill reminiscing about the past. Jo, of course, is talking whilst I type onto my iPad. She says she can still hear my voice as I tap away, and this cheers me up. We discuss the chapter I wrote about my first year of teaching, which triggers off more old memories, and soon we are giggling away the way we used to in the staffroom.

'God, do you remember Boring Ted?' she asks. 'He talked so slowly that I always wanted to finish his sentences.'

'Oh, yes, and Mrs Dobby, who told me she kept a bottle of Scotch in her locker for medicinal purposes, if ever I was in need of it.' You'd be sacked now, I type, thinking back to some of the things we did in those days; the Friday pub lunches, parties with sixth formers and wild, staff drinking sessions.

'And Dick Plumly, who told you he kept control with his charisma! Nigel was always taking the piss out of him after that.' Jo laughed.

'And then we found out he'd failed his probationary year!'

Later we move on to the people in our book clubs, and the novels we've recently enjoyed. Having admitted to being total book snobs, we frequently roll our eyes about various popular overrated novels. To impress Jo, I click onto the Kindle app on my iPad, only to discover to my horror that what I am currently reading is *Fifty Shades of Grey* – a best selling, mummy-porn book, allegedly flying off the shelves in Asda, if you believe the hype.

'Lindy, are you really reading this?' She laughs. I know she's teasing me after all my crowing about quality literature.

No, no, I mean, yes, but only so I can say I've read it, I type. 'It's crap, really badly written.'

We both hoot with laughter.

'Wait till I tell Paul.'

'No, Jo, no!' I type. It's research.

We're off, shrieking again.

Later I buy two literary books from the bookshop, making sure she notes the authors, and at home unwrap Jo's present to me, *The Writing Diary of Virginia Woolf.* Wonderful.

I fight off serious happy face-licking from Scrappy then read again the Facebook message from Omari, one of my ex-students from Cheshunt School (2005–2009), that I have received in the morning and once more glow with pride. I taught Omari GCSE English, then A-level English Literature and he was also in my sixth-form tutor group.

Hi Miss, extraordinary news!

I got a first class honours degree and am receiving an award for 'best marketing project', an award bestowed by the union the best dissertation. I have also been selected for inclusion in the 2012/2013 edition of 'Future Leaders' magazine, which is sponsored by Barclays and charts the top 100 black graduates. No celebration would be complete without you, so I would be honoured if you could attend my graduation.

'Try stopping me.' I reply, tears pouring down my cheeks, thinking of Omari and how far he has come.

I remember:

The determined sixteen-year-old GCSE student, who insisted we did regular, timed essays and would bounce up to me in the corridor a day later to ask if I had marked them. (I even used to mark essays on Saturday afternoon, not daring to disappoint him!)

Then the A-level student who once said, 'I love English, it's so deep, Miss, isn't it?'

The young man, who with his friend Xavier, helped me out at open evenings by enticing nervous little visiting Year-6 students to write poems. The parents stood in awe at his entertaining and charismatic performance whilst the children sucked on boiled sweets and wrote 'powerful adjectives' onto a whiteboard describing taste and texture.

The memory of my tears in the garden, when his mum phoned and told me he'd been stabbed and that he'd like me to visit him in hospital.

And then the angry, vengeful survivor – his mind tormented for months by what had happened to him.

But Omari came through it, as I knew he would, and now. Now…

Steve Jobs, the same age as me, and who died this year, talked of making way for the younger generation, but as with my own beloved sons, I am very sad that I won't live to see Omari's progress.

Letter

•

Lastly, a piece from Keith Rose, who along with Jeni, Simon, Monica, Lindsey, Richard, Mary and Marion encouraged me on writing weekends for more than twenty years. Without this wonderful group of people, this memoir would never have been written.

We always knew when you'd reached the back door. An explosion of goodwill and unlikely stories surrounded your arrival like a fanfare. You seemed to have the knack of catching the train that would be delayed, or getting the taxi whose driver couldn't read a map. Where this might have flustered others – reduced them to tears, even – you accepted it all as part of life's interesting chaos, noisily regaling us with the day's doings once you had a glass of wine in your hand.

And then you wrote. My, how you wrote. Never has

one finger tapped out so much prose for so long. Was it always in longhand first time round? We seemed to be witnesses to an endless supply of wire-bound notebooks, full of ink and story. The classrooms, the streets, the pelting corridors, the twists and unfairness of ruthless adolescent lives – they are all there on the pages of your novels. I am never quite sure which tale it is that you are sharing when you read to us – the whole *oeuvre* seems like something out of Balzac, because your renditions from the sofa always take us into Lindy's world, a complete world full of tears and grotesque laughs which leap out from your mind as if it was so obvious that this teeming life could never be simple or dull.

And so we walked the corridors with you, rejoiced in your rough dialogue, marvelled at the hard knocks, and remembered what it was like to be 16 again. I never really knew how you did it. I just recognised honesty when I heard it.

When it came to the writing exercises, you'd be very happy to take the plunge – but not before some remonstration about the instructions or some coarse joke about a possibility which had flashed through your head. We'd laugh and feel glad to be alive… then silence for ten minutes, as we scratched our thoughts on paper, interrupted by the chimes of the clock or someone knocking over their coffee.

What has kept us at it? I guess we all love words, and more importantly we give full respect to the power of words – how they can fascinate, destroy, encourage, or amuse. And you have been proof that the words don't have to be written down to have such power: your eye-popping tales and cackling bits of autobiography have entertained and absorbed us all, as we scoffed the pasta at Oak Farm or downed the chardonnay at Booton.

And now you can no longer join us at our gatherings. You are 'indisposed', as the theatre managers would say. My homage to our weekend word-smithing – and your important part in it all – only serves to underscore the unfairness of your illness. Not that unfairness will be a new concept to you; so much of your writing has dealt with difficulty and the wrongness of things. Nevertheless, your situation is hard, very hard. And you are brave; as I am sure many people have told you. One week you are trolling along thinking that MND is shorthand for the tale of Hermia and Lysander and Bottom's dream, and the next week another MND plunges you into your own terrors in 'a wood outside Athens' – with no obvious happy ending for you or your family.

I wonder if the schoolchildren realised how lucky they were to have you as their teacher. You would never call them children, of course; you respected them too much for that. But did they fathom the reserves of energy you must have drawn upon for them? Have they yet under-stood your inconspicuous commitment to their progress and well-being? Perhaps not, but then you didn't do it for the recognition.

I am glad to know that you are still writing your story, Lindy. Include whatever you like of the above in your ac-count. We miss your presence at our weekends. It really isn't the same without you. But even if you can no longer hold your own amongst us inveterate talkers, we want you to go on writing (sharing what you can). I hope you know that we all recognise you for what you are – a writer.

That time of year thou mayst in me behold
When yellow leaves, or none, or few, do hang
Upon those boughs which shake against the cold,
Bare ruined choirs, where late the sweet birds sang.

In me thou see'st the twilight of such day
As after sunset fadeth in the west;
Which by and by black night doth take away,
Death's second self, that seals up all in rest.

In me thou see'st the glowing of such fire,
That on the ashes of his youth doth lie,
As the death-bed, whereon it must expire,
Consumed with that which it was nourish'd by.

This thou perceiv'st, which makes thy love more strong,
To love that well, which thou must leave ere long.

William Shakespeare
Sonnet 73

Chapter Twenty-Four

What Lindy Did Next

•

Whenever you ask my eighty-seven-year-old dad how he is, his reply is almost always, 'still afloat', a phrase I have recently taken over for myself. So here I am, in June 2013, 'still afloat', although some days I feel much more like I'm drowning. But hey, today it's a beautiful, sunny day and I am celebrating the fact that I have defied the prognosis given to me last May, a result of my perseverance with the breathing ventilator, a.k.a. the Hannibal Lecter Mask, which I am plugged into every night. At the moment, death does not seem imminent. However, given the fact that most MND patients end up totally paralyzed, I can't get too carried away with positivity.

Typing is now also very difficult, as my hands have turned into two disobedient creatures whose fingers are curling inwards towards the palm. These precious hands, which have been my loyal companions for fifty-seven years, are deserting me and leaving in their place two weak claws which are pretty damn useless. I am also very worried about my legs, wondering how much longer I will be able to manage the stairs as Mildred has her nails into them now and I can see the muscles beginning to waste.

Recently, we have been having discussions about stair-lifts, although discussion isn't a very accurate description of a situation that neither Gareth nor I ever imagined happening. So there is a lot of prevaricating – that's Gareth, and crying – that's me. I feel unspeakably sad about losing my own room on the first floor if our stairs are too narrow for a lift. Trapped downstairs, I will have to face up to the fact that I will never sit here at my own desk again, never be in the place I have written my diary, prepared lessons, composed my novels and marked work. This little room is part of me and giving it up is unbearable.

On certain days it still seems unbelievable that I have morphed into this feeble helpless creature kept alive by a plastic tube, unable to do so many ordinary tasks that healthy people take for granted. In fact, my house has now turned into an assault course, with a gradually lengthening list of things that I can no longer do. I'll give you an example: a packet of cat food. Before Mildred, I could rip those foil packets open with a quick hand movement. Now, using two hands and a large pair of scissors, it takes me a painful five minutes to cut the top off. Light switches have to be operated with my head, and anything that needs me to lift up an arm – forget it.

However, when asked by a close friend last week if I would like to travel to Switzerland and end it all, my answer was a definite 'no'. There are lots of things I can still enjoy despite my disabled state. So, to counterbalance the negative, here are things I can still do:

Read
Watch films
Hear
Touch
Smell
Walk
Write (just about)
Enjoy being with friends

You can see how hard I am trying to be positive and not depress the hell out of you, but it is a daily battle to fight off total despair.

Mentally, my mood stays at about minus 5 most of the time, occasionally rising to 0, though there have been odd times when I have actually rated myself as feeling almost cheerful, say about plus 5. But far more commonly, I plunge to a definite minus 20. Sorry to disappoint you, but I have not accepted my illness with a peaceful serenity; I am still raging, still feeling sorry for myself and still being temperamental.

At night I often dream that I am eating and drinking. Some mornings, when I wake up, I lie and remember the tastes and textures of some of my favourite meals. I don't think I have actually eaten any 'real' food for well over a year, but daily life revolves around eating, and sometimes photos of food on Facebook drive me into a frenzy of longing. A few weeks ago we met some friends in our local just as they were about to be served up an enormous roast-dinner. The tantalizing smell of chicken and potatoes was so overpowering that I had to restrain myself from bursting into tears and running out. One of them managed to mumble 'Oh, sorry, Lindy', before complaining that she couldn't possibly manage to eat so much. The other two chomped their way through their meals without a word.

In situations like that, I feel shut away from the world and often find myself wishing that, in my previous healthy existence, I had had a more balanced attitude to food, instead of constantly denying myself things in an attempt to stay slim. Embarking on my first diet at fourteen was the beginning of a neurotic obsession with my weight, and a lifetime of depriving myself of enough to eat. For about fifteen years, my lunch was a small pot of cottage cheese, a cup of slim-a-soup and two pieces of fruit. A sandwich, in my eyes, was looked upon as sinful, although I did allow myself to eat toast in the morning. If I could live my life again, I would definitely eat a lot more cake.

When I was teaching, I hardly watched television at all; there was simply no time. At seven p.m., I'd pour myself a large glass of white wine, lug my two heavy school bags up to my work room and sit down to mark and prepare lessons for the next day, often surrounded by our two cats who would periodically walk across students' work, leaving muddy footprints. Meanwhile, Gareth would be cooking our supper. This arrangement suited us both. I had time to sort out my schoolwork, and he could cook food he wanted to eat rather than my semi-vegetarian concoctions which had never been very well received. (We'd once had a massive row over my cod-in-cheese-sauce which I served up on our wedding anniversary.) He also accused me, unfairly I thought, of reading books whilst the food burnt.

Anyway, my former life was very, very hectic but now, now I have time to watch box sets for the first time and have worked my way through two series of *Homeland*, two series of *Fresh Meat*, four series of *Breaking Bad* – just waiting for fifth one to be released – and have now started on *Dexter*. Because my eldest son Robbie works shifts, we have been able to watch these together, which has been great for both of us, and we spend ages discussing people's characters and what motivates them.

In my life before MND, I was very partial to a few glasses of white wine and must have clocked up a good few thousand hours nattering with various friends whilst slurping away. (If you are a doctor please look away now.) In my new life, as a member of the MND club, I still go out to pubs but now I syringe booze into my PEG as: a) I can't lift a glass to my lips and b) I can't swallow very well. I have initiated several of my friends in the art of 'whooshing', the verb which perfectly describes the way the alcohol shoots down the plastic tube and straight into my stomach.

Since I have been unable to talk, I listen much more carefully to people. Before, I would have been desperate to get a word in and had to restrain myself many a time from interrupting conversations. And I know this is going to sound a bit New Age and Hippyish, but I feel that I sense things about people we know, as if my intuition has been intensified. I can definitely, like dogs and horses, smell fear; fear of what to say, or not say. Fear of my illness. Fear of my death. In certain moods I dare to make flippant jokes about my funeral, guaranteed to make some of Gareth's friends turn pale.

But enough of this rambling. I'd like to explain how this book came into being.

In October 2011, I enrolled on a memoir-writing course run by Faber and tutored by Gillian Slovo, after having started to write about my illness the year before. The structure of the weekly meetings was for each group member to volunteer to have their writing assessed by the group and the second half of the two-hour session would be given over to discussion about the piece. I wanted to get this out of the way, so I volunteered to be the second 'victim'.

Having e-mailed my first chapter to Gillian, who distributed it, I anxiously entered the Faber building the following week, wondering whether I might have written total crap. I signed in, stepped into the lift where a sprightly, rather glamorous woman said, 'Oh, are you Lindy? I loved your writing.' I was genuinely shocked. Had she mixed me up with someone else? But no. The rest of the group were enthusiastic too, I was amazed. I'd had countless rejections from publishers and agents over the years and, though I love writing, I wasn't really sure if I was any good. The course ended at Christmas and I carried on writing encouraged by all the people I had sent my chapters to. Untimely death is a great motivator, there's simply no time to waste, and so I just kept going.

But something completely unexpected was about to happen. A few days before Christmas, I received a message from an old boyfriend, Keith McMullan, who had found out about my diagnosis. (Irish Keith in Chapter 18 of the book.) I had not seen him for thirty-two years, even though we don't live that far from each other. In January, we met up for coffee and a catch up.

News of careers, marriage and children followed before I tentatively mentioned my writing and he told me he would love to read it. Soon, I was sending him my chapters on a regular basis and we would meet to discuss it. His pearls of wisdom were invaluable, given his experience of editing (albeit for alien economic-type publications), and gradually the book began to take shape. You know, dear Keith, that I can never thank you enough, for everything.

In December 2012, Sue Hollick, the woman in the lift who had complimented me on my writing, hosted a soirée with everyone from the memoir-writing course. What I hadn't realized was that she was a Baroness (when you have spent your working life in North London comprehensives, you can't help being impressed) and lived in the most amazing house in Notting Hill Gate. Of course, I wasn't able to eat the delicious canapés or guzzle the champagne, but I feasted instead on the praise lavished on me – a wonderful evening.

It's so strange how a life you envisaged going in one direction can suddenly completely change. Four years ago I was thinking of retirement and grandchildren, and then came the shock of a terminal illness and everything was thrown into chaos. This was never the book I ever imagined writing and although I am very proud of it, I'd much rather be healthy.

Pinned on the wall next to my computer is a card that says, 'Today is a Gift', but like most of us, I spent a lot of time in my previous life either looking back or trying to imagine the future. But now I really try my best to seize each day and live in the present which, when you think about it, is all any of us really has anyway.

'Hold on a goddamn minute, kiddo.'

'Oh, here we go. I knew you couldn't let me finish my chapter without poking your nose in.'

Mildred is standing next to me peering at the screen,

'It's just… .hmm… well, hun, it just doesn't sound like you. I mean where's the raging? The crying? The self-pity, for God's sake?'

'Okay, okay, I get the message. I was just trying to end things on a positive note… even if… well it's a bit cheesy… how about this then.'

•

I am sitting here in my little room looking at the sky. Dusk is approaching and the last of the sun's rays are lighting up the rolling, grey clouds that drift over the rooftops. So many amazing and unexpected things have happened to me over the last two years. Despite my deteriorating health, Mildred has brought great love into my life. That's the thing about dying, it shows you the people who are brave enough to cope with all the sadness and still be there with you.

Thunder is rumbling now and cheerful voices echo from a nearby garden. A grey, pink-tinted cloud rolls towards the chimney pots. Yes, night is coming and more than ever since becoming ill, each evening reminds me that every day must end.

'Is this it then? Jeez I was really worried you were going to get too serious and spiritual there for a moment. Though I like the way you finally had to admit that I do have a good side.'

Mildred puts her fingers on my shoulder and squeezes gently. She is dressed in grey: her sleek, dark hair falling neatly over one shoulder. She is holding a small bunch of black roses.

'You ready?'

'No. I... I...' Silent tears roll down my face.

Mildred turns towards me and dabs gently at my cheeks. The handkerchief shimmers in the fading light.

And then suddenly, I'm standing in the middle of a stage lit up by a spotlight, huge images of my book surround me. In the front row I can see Gareth (with Scrappy), Robbie and Owen, dad, Viv and Karey, and they are all smiling proudly at me as I stand with a copy of my book and take a bow. And then I see my friends, people I've met over the years; people I've laughed with, cried with, got drunk with and they are all clapping and cheering me. Me! Miraculously transformed into my former healthy self for my last great performance.

'Thank you, thank you everyone.' I wave and bow again, savouring the sound of my old familiar voice restored for its final moments.

And then once more I smile at the crowd, and cry and flutter my beautiful butterfly wings, as the curtain begins to move slowly, very slowly, across the stage. I want to stay here for just a bit longer, to make every second I have left of my time on earth as bright and as dazzling as it can be. I look across at my beloved family for the very last time.

And then it's over. The curtain has closed and Mildred is standing next to me. She places the roses down by my feet and reaches out for my hand.

'That was some send off, kid,' she whispers gently.

A soft wind blows the coldness towards us as we walk back together into the wings. I stop for a minute, the urge to turn around almost unbearable.

'It's your time sweetie,' whispers Mildred gently, 'keep going.'

The darkness opens up in front of us.

I don't look back.

Winning the Alternative Lottery

by Gareth Jones

•

We all think, wouldn't it be great to win the lottery. It won't change my life we say but it will. So be very careful what you wish for.

In some sort of a perverse way, getting MND is like winning an alternative lottery. It's an extremely rare illness and it will change your life forever whether you want it to or not. All you have known before disappears, to be replaced by a daily journey with some occasional wins but more unfortunately regular losses, of things we all take for granted. The disease progresses in a completely unpredictable way, at an unknown speed with no road map available for the journey it is taking you on.

To win the UK Lotto jackpot you need to match all six main numbers from the range 1 to 49. There are 13,983,816 possible combinations of six numbers from 49 numbers so the lottery odds of winning the jackpot are 1 in 13,983,816 pretty high but we can all dream. So what are the odds of suffering cancer or MND then? Well, more than one in three people in the UK will develop some form of cancer during their lifetime but the incidence or number of people who will develop MND each year is about two people in every 100,000. The prevalence or number of people living with MND at any one time is approximately 5,000, so you can see that compared to cancer there is only a minute chance of contracting it.

Motor Neurone Disease is a term that leaves you cold. It sounds bad you know its bad but it's rare. Hardly any one has it and although of course you sympathise with them, they are just the unlucky ones, not lucky like you. You don't really know about it and in truth don't want to either. As our son Owen once said to Lindy, 'It's not like you wake up every morning thinking, thank God I don't have MND.'

Doctors cannot tell you what will happen, which part of your body will stop functioning next so this negative lottery prize carries on its merry way with its individual destructive path. It's not like cancer, which although we all fear it, people do survive. We know a great deal about its symptoms, how fast it will move and our chances of remission though this is not to play down the terrible effects of cancer. My father died of lung cancer, my mother had breast cancer and Lindy's own mother died of non-Hodgkins Lymphoma, so we understand how it devastates lives and at some level almost suspect, in our healthy lives, that it will probably get us in the end but at some time unspecified in the future.

But MND has a life of its own. Everybody who has this disease is special, it's personal, it attacks different parts of the body and no one really knows where and when it will strike, only how devastating it will be. It slowly or quickly changes lives, with random destruction of the motor neurons, leaving the sensory neurons undamaged along with the personality and intellect of the sufferer. How cruel to see and understand what's happening to your own body

Lindy is very special to us, wonderfully unique, lively, vivacious and eccentric (in a very positive way!!). I could go on forever but I will never get close to describing the person who I have been so lucky to meet and through thick and thin remain together, still so happy with and easy in each other's company after being together for over 30 years, over half our lifetimes. It has not all been easy but we did it.

We have some time left though we don't know how much so we still try to do as many things as we can though it is getting much harder for Lindy now. This is our time together no matter how much this fucking disease tries to come between us, we will not let it until eventually, as always, everything changes...

We had plans and dreams of an Arcadian retirement with a dog somewhere never specified - Lindy loves the city and me the small town - but it was going to happen somehow, sometime. Now though plans have changed. We are staying in London and got our dog immediately after Lindy was diagnosed. We both felt so sorry for the majority of dogs at Battersea, but when we saw Scrappy he was so full of energy, friendliness and especially LIFE, we knew he was the dog for us and so he joined our family. Robbie who is not over keen on dogs loves him now although both sons tell me that he's the favourite son! Well he does not answer back, ask for money or stay out late!! He has helped us all deal with this, as he is always so happy it's infectious and even when we get down his wagging tail and cheeky shoe stealing habit makes it all easier to bear. He also helps Lindy some days to get out of the house and stay active as he wants a walk and a squirrel chase which should definitely I think be an Olympic sport – a nailed-on Gold for Team GB.

Lindy touched so many people in her long and fulfilling career in teaching. She was patient (at school anyway, not necessarily at home!!), caring and dedicated, not interested in the career ladder and although she became Head of English she loved the cut and thrust of the classroom telling me vivid stories of lessons and some of the characters who she nurtured and supported, allowing them to develop into real human beings. She highlighted their skills and praised their achievements, not just as in the blinkered academic requirements of obsessive government targets, but as people with individual personalities and strengths.

As she got older she felt tired a lot and in 2010 when her voice became a little slurred I used to joke when I got home that it was, 'a bit early for the pop', as she was partial to a glass of wine with the marking. Little did I suspect that we were in fact just about to win the alternative lottery.

The written word both reading and writing is a passion for Lindy. I can remember on various holidays in foreign parts, Lindy's head wearing a book like a sunhat. I was frustrated by this but as always, gave a running commentary on the sights and sounds of our various tours to cultural and historical sites whilst she, oblivious to everything but the words on the pages of what ever novel she was reading at that time, ignored me.

She had a fantastic loud and infectious laugh and we teased her about her conversations with various people she met, telling them her life story, she was so sociable and lively. When she returned from a trip to Canada to visit Karey when Robyn was born we went to collect her at Gatwick and even at an early age Robbie – now a pilot – was interested in planes and wanted to know what route Lindy had taken going to Canada. Lindy, weary after the trip said, 'Oh I don't know, over Germany I think.' Novels, yes please, geography, *nein danke*!

Wine, her tipple of choice, has become too sharp and thin as swallowing has got worse but she has discovered Baileys, its texture and thickness helping her to swallow. It is painful but ultimately uplifting to watch her still fight to enjoy her Baileys in a whisky tumbler with one piece of ice, as she still carries on drinking and socialising, making the best of the circumstances

The loss of her voice is a particularly cruel experience for Lindy as she was so enthusiastically vocal and full of words and laughter. Writing has become her lifeline now her speech is unintelligible and has taken on a life of its own, not only for her serious writing but also for when we have our cosy little 'chats' in bars. (She now has to write everything down on an iPad.) We still seem to think the same things, knowing what each other is thinking (we are a lot of things but I don't think anyone would call us boring). It does not stop us bickering though, something we have always done. Some people could never understand how we could be so happy when we argued so much but only on the trivial things, in life we are very different people but oh so similar!! Our moral and political values are almost identical and it makes me feel so good to be with someone who cares and stands up for their own feelings and ideas. I am selfish and also a little opinionated (A LITTLE!) so need to be told in no uncertain terms when to get off.

Communicating now can be very frustrating for Lindy who knows exactly what she wants to say or do and she even resorted to trying to kick me some weeks ago out of sheer anger and frustration as she was trying to say something very simple but I did not understand and kept getting the wrong end of the stick. We would have looked a merry couple in what appeared like a weird dance round the sitting room me leading to avoid the flailing kicks aimed at my shins!!!

The iPad has now replaced the rather heavy and untrendy looking lightwriter which we were originally given by the National Health who have been fantastic in supporting us all throughout this living nightmare. Our lives and horizons are maybe narrowing but we are trying not to give up.

When Warren Zevron was asked what advice he had about life after he was diagnosed with terminal cancer he said, 'Enjoy every sandwich.' A good motto to live by.

The shin kicking is absolutely true but Gareth has missed out the build up, which was a series of frenzied tappings onto my iPad, followed by gasping screams of frustration and hysterical crying as I could not make myself understood.

Motor Neurone Disease (MND) is a progressive disease that attacks the motor neurones, or nerves, in the brain and spinal cord. This means messages gradually stop reaching muscles, which leads to weakness and wasting.

MND can affect how you walk, talk, eat, drink and breathe. However, not all symptoms necessarily happen to everyone and it is unlikely they will all develop at the same time, or in any specific order. Although there is currently no cure for MND, symptoms can be managed to help you achieve the best possible quality of life.

It is difficult to be exact, but statistics for Motor Neurone Disease tell us that:

- It can affect any adult at any age but most people diagnosed with the disease are over the age of 40, with the highest incidence occurring between the ages of 50 and 70

- Men are affected approximately twice as often as women

- The incidence or number of people who will develop MND each year is about two people in every 100,000

- The prevalence or number of people living with MND at any one time is approximately seven in every 100,000

The Motor Neurone Disease Association is the only national charity in England, Wales and Northern Ireland that funds and promotes global research into the disease and provides support for people affected by MND. We now have 3,000 volunteers in England, Wales and Northern Ireland and 150-plus paid staff, all dedicated to improving the lives of people affected by MND, now and in the future.

For further information on the work of the MND Association, visit: www.mndassociation.org

Motor Neurone Disease Association
PO Box 246, Northampton NN1 2PR

Published in 2014 in Great Britain by:

Ashgrove Publishing

an imprint of:

Hollydata Publishers Ltd
27 John Street
London
WC1N 2BX

ISBN 978 185398 184 5

Book design by Brad Thompson

Printed and bound in England